FREE INDEED

FREE TO LIVE A LIFE OF OBEDIENCE

MICHAEL DOW

BURNING
ONES

Dedication

I dedicate this book to my wife, Anna, and two children, Ariyah and Josiah. I love you with all of my heart and am thankful to God for the great joy and strength you add to my life.

Table of Contents

Introduction

What is obedience? By definition, obedience is simply: compliance with an order, request, or law, or submission to another's authority. Today the word "obedience" has developed a negative connotation. When you mention the word "obey," people begin to cringe because it doesn't seem to have a positive side to it. You hear things like: kids must obey their parents; you must obey the law of the land; obey your doctors' orders, and so on. Anywhere obedience is mentioned there is this great sense that it involves some type of dominating authoritative figure that is out to impose their will or enforce their authority by power.

In the day that Jesus walked the earth Caesar was the king of the most powerful government in the land, the Roman Empire, and considered to be lord as well. It was a common thing to hear, "Caesar is lord," come out of people's mouths. The Roman Empire ruled the people by overpowering them. Caesar's policy was, in my own interpretation, bow down or die. Caesar suppressed the identity of the people and forced them into a place of submission. If you didn't adhere to Caesar's demands you could very easily, and most likely, find yourself losing your life by being beaten to death or fed to wild beasts. Obedience to the Roman government system was something that everybody would have been familiar with.

Unlike Caesar's policy of bow down or die, Jesus came with a much different approach. Jesus wasn't looking to suppress people's identity by overpowering them, but rather to cause them to come alive to their identity by empowering them to believe in whom the Father had made them to be. Jesus wasn't demanding that men bow down or die; instead, because men had died to themselves, they began to bow down to the One who was truly the King of Kings and the Lord of Lords.

It would be safe to say that Jesus and Caesar had different strategies in getting men to invest into this thing called obedience. However, I would argue that true obedience could never be motivated by fear or manipulation. What am I saying? What I am saying is this: in order for it to be complete obedience, which is wholehearted submission, it must be done with just that, my whole heart. If there were no other option presented to me I would not say that you have my complete wholehearted obedience. If I were told, "Do this or die," I may do it, but not because I really want to serve, but because I do not want to lose my life.

Being motivated by a negative consequence is never going to cause my heart to come alive to the point where I am wholly invested in obedience out of true devotion and submission. Let me say this again, fear will never be an adequate motivator for obedience. You may have people doing what you want them to, but they will never love you; you will never capture their hearts.

What is an adequate motivator for obedience? I would argue that obedience must be birthed out of love. To me, obedience is an expression of love. Obedience is love in action. Jesus said in John 14:23-24, "Jesus replied, 'Anyone who loves me will obey my teaching. My Father will love them, and we will come to them and make our home with them. Anyone who does not love me will not obey my teaching. These words you hear are not my own; they belong to the Father who sent me.'"[1] This seems to make it very clear; obedience is an issue of love. Those who love Me, Jesus says, will obey My teaching and those who do not love Me will not obey. There doesn't seem to be much gray area with what Jesus is saying.

---

[1] John 14:23-24 (NIV)

If obedience is a love issue, whenever I find myself having issues with obedience, I don't need to try and obey more; I need to fall in love more. Let me put it this way: if you talk about obedience with those who are not in love, it becomes works; it turns into a yoke of bondage, a list of things I have to do. But, if you have the same talk with people that are head over heels in love, it becomes a delight. The psalmist says in Psalm 40:8, "I delight to do Your will, O my God; Your Law is within my heart."[2]

When I fell in love with my wife, nobody had to tell me that there were certain things I was supposed to do in order to express that love. When I fell head over heels in love with my wife I went out of my way at every opportunity that presented itself in order for me to express my love for her. In fact, I went looking for opportunities to express my love for her; money didn't matter, time didn't matter, the way that I looked to others didn't matter. The only thing that I knew was that my heart had been ravished with such great intensity and with everything within me it naturally pushed me to do something!

My greatest desire is that you fall head over heels in love with Jesus in a fresh way that changes your life. I pray that you love Him with such great intensity that it causes you to say yes to Him every moment of the day. Having your heart softened to where you say yes to Him

---

[2] Ps. 40:8 (NASB)

continually throughout the day is what it is all about. I have always wanted to cultivate a "yes" on the inside for Jesus. I am not so much worried about a twenty-year plan, a ten-year vision, or what I will be doing a year from now, as much as I am

My greatest desire is that you fall head over heels in love with Jesus in a fresh way that changes your life.

concerned with keeping my heart softened to the Lord and continually having a "yes" to Him. I know many that have a fancy multiyear vision yet do not have a "yes" to Him in the present.

As long as I have a "yes" in the moment I don't really need to be stressed out over what will be five years from now, because my "yes" moment by moment, if kept, will always land me right where I need to be as I walk with Him and love Him. I want you to walk with Him for the rest of your days and love Him more. I want you to see the One who offered Himself for you in a real way that causes you to lovingly and wholeheartedly surrender your life and deny yourself to be found in His pursuit. Following Jesus isn't about a to-do list; it's about a love encounter! What could possibly be a better way to spend the rest of your life, than in love? He is waiting for you!

1

Setting the Stage

J esus says that for any man to come after Him he must first deny himself.[3] I find it really intentional on the part of Jesus that the very entryway to discipleship and a life of following Him is the hardest thing for any of us to do. Denying ourselves is not something that comes naturally; it's not something that we are instinctively prone to pursue; yet, nevertheless, Jesus starts there! Jesus wants all of you, not just the pieces you are willing to hand over. Our culture tells us to look out for number one. We live in an individualistic society that teaches the pursuit of

---

[3] Matt. 16:24 (NIV)

whatever may make the individual happy. This may come as breaking news to you, but you were not created to merely be happy. You were created for more than chasing after temporary moments of happiness. Happiness is conditional. You have got to see that there is more to life than the effortless pursuit of yourself.

How different would your life be if you really surrendered it all to Jesus? What would your life look like if you passionately and radically abandoned yourself in order to find the abundant life that is promised by Him?[4] It is not good enough just to know about Him. He wants us to know Him, and know Him deeply and intimately. He wants us to know Him in a way that will profoundly reshape all that we are and all that we desire. This invitation into abundant life in John 10:10 is not an offering for more material things; it is an offer for more of Him! Have you connected with this place? Have you realized that there is more to Jesus than whatever amount you have become content with? Jesus is greater than the little box we tend to put Him in. For all eternity we will behold His great-

> **It is not good enough just to know about Him. He wants us to know Him, and know Him deeply and intimately.**

---

[4] John 10:10 (NIV)

ness and continue to be awed at the splendor of His majesty.

What makes this Jesus so worthy of an individual that He would be able to demand all of someone's life? Have you ever sat to really consider why Jesus would feel able to issue the invitation to men to relinquish one's life into His leading? I have; I had to. I had to get revelation for myself of the greatness of Jesus that the Bible speaks about if I was ever going to be able to fully invest in His pursuit.

John 3:16 says, "For God so loved the world that he gave his one and only Son, that whoever believes in Him might not perish but have eternal life." Isaiah 9:6-7 says of Him, "For to us a child is born, to us a son is given, and the government will be on his shoulders. And he will be called Wonderful Counselor, Mighty God, Everlasting Father, and Prince of Peace. Of the increase of his government and peace there will be no end. He will reign on David's throne and over his kingdom, establishing and upholding it with justice and righteousness from that time on and forever. The zeal of the LORD Almighty will accomplish this." Isaiah 53:10-11 says, "Yet it was the Lord's will to crush him and cause him to suffer, and though the Lord makes his life a guilt offering, he will see his offspring and prolong his days, and the will of the Lord will prosper in his hand. After the suffering of his soul, he will see the light [of life] and be satisfied; by his knowledge my righteous servant will justify many, and he will bear their iniquities."

We could go on and on through the Scriptures to bring to life the beauty of Jesus, but we will stop there for a moment. Do you realize that perfection came and took your place? Jesus, heaven's best offering, the King of Kings and the Lord of Lords, God's only Son came and died in your place in order to pay the penalty for your sin. The book of 2 Corinthians tells us that God made him who had no sin to be sin for us, so that in him we might become the righteousness of God.[5] Your sin has been paid for with the price of a life, and not just any life; the life of God Himself.

Stop and consider for a moment that God came and died for you. This isn't just something in history that randomly happened and has some sort of application for you; this is personal and this is for you. Jesus was whipped, beaten, and brutalized in order for you to have an invitation to life in Him. The penalty of sin had left us to the pursuit of wickedness and ourselves.

Jesus came at a hopeless time when it seemed that all was lost, and He laid down His life in order to repair the breach. Jesus clung to the cross in hopes that one day you might cling to Him. His nail-pierced hands would not

---

[5] 2 Cor. 5:21

release the cross in hopes that you might one day lay hold of Him and refuse to let go. In relentless love, Jesus willingly embraced the cross, scorning its shame, for the joy that was set before Him—that joy was you!

Have you embraced this truth? I am not asking if you have ever heard this. I am not even asking if you simply agree or amen what I am saying. Have you embraced this? It is one thing to grab hold of something intellectually and carry around a head knowledge that doesn't produce anything different in our everyday living. It is another thing to really embrace it with your heart and allow it to be woven into the fabric of who you are.

The One that came and walked among us over two thousand years ago wants to walk with you today. The One that opened blind eyes, cleansed the leper, freed the crippled, and allowed the lame to dance wants to join Himself to your life and dwell with you. The best heaven has to offer has offered His life for you, and has now offered His life to you if you would be willing to lay it all down and pursue Him. If any man would come after Me…this is the intended invitation to a lifelong pursuit of a person.

Don't get this distorted and think that we are simply to pursue a behavioral change or certain spiritual disciplines. We are to pursue Jesus! It is not enough to acquire a fancy list of spiritual practices and disciplines if they are not leading us to touch Him, leading us to a greater experience of His presence in our lives. Anything that is not leading us to greater life in Him is leading to a dead end and needs to be cut out of our lives.

There is nothing wrong with a routine or regular spiritual habits, but if it becomes more about the routine than the One that the routine is leading us to, we need to examine why we are doing what we are doing. Jesus is not simply after an appearance in our lives, the appearance of spirituality. He desires reality and He has made this reality available to those that would seek Him. We seek Him with great expectation of finding Him; we seek Him because He desires to be found!

Jesus longs for the day when you would come to the end of yourself and simply surrender. Will you surrender? What is holding you back? What has been worthy enough of a cause that it would keep you from committing your all to Him? We really do only have this one life to live, and I would encourage you to live it for something that is worth the price Jesus paid in dying for you. Go after Him!

2

Unlikely Candidate

There I found myself, in a love encounter with Jesus that wrecked me and literally changed my entire life. I stood weeping uncontrollably in the strength of His embrace at the end of a Sunday night service at the altar of a church in central Florida. This may sound like the norm for some, but this is not what I would have expected in a million years for me. Jesus would accept me? Jesus would welcome me into His Kingdom? Someone with a past like mine was not supposed to be able to come before the King, much less be embraced by Him and called His own. Yet there I stood, weeping uncontrollably, overcome by a love so unrelenting and genuine that it disarmed every wall and controllable barrier that my heart had erected over years of tough places in life.

To rewind for just a moment, I was not even at church that night intentionally seeking God; I was there to get into a fight. I was carrying a backpack full of drugs that I had picked up earlier that afternoon and was determined to just handle this little issue of business and get back to life as I knew it to be. But, you see, it is in those moments where we feel like we have everything put together for ourselves that Jesus knocks us off of our horse and redirects our steps. I didn't know it at the time, but God had set me up by taking me to that service. God had greater plans for that night than the little fight I thought I was trying to get into.

Just turning twenty-one years old a few weeks prior, I was the most unlikely candidate for the Lord to accept. My parents separated right before I turned sixteen, and life, as I knew it, had experienced drastic changes in many ways. I found myself out of the house and living out on the streets; getting expelled from high school during my senior year; in and out of jail several times; committed to a life of drugs, partying, violence; a five-year suspension on my driver's license; diseased; and living with no hope. This lifestyle choice consumed the next several years of my life. I know what it is like to look up at the sky and wonder if there really is a God. I know what it is like to wonder why life has to be a certain way and feel like there is nothing you can do in order to produce a different outcome than the one you are currently experiencing.

Because of where and how I was living I believe that a person's behavior is not always the greatest indicator, nor does it always point to concrete evidence, of what is in an individual's heart. Even when I was at my absolute worst, when I was a part of things that I am certainly not proud of today, I would walk the streets at night drunk and high, or sit up and just cry out to a God that I didn't even know really existed. I grew up with a mild understanding about church, never really a great priority in our life. I can count the number of times I went to church in my youth on one hand. My mother had a form of Catholicism but nothing to the point that it had a major impact on my life at any point. I had questioned the existence of God many times, not really having a framework to even interpret my own thoughts about who or what He would be all about.

I had never opened a Bible and read it for myself in all of my twenty-one years of living. Yet, at my absolute worst, I would cry out to God on many occasions and with everything that I knew how, wanting to know why my life had to be a certain way. You see, I thought that God created some to enjoy the luxuries and pleasures of life, and others were created in order to endure suffering and hellish-type existences. My life was one, that up until that point, I had definitely identified with the latter of the two options. I wanted to be different. I wanted to change. I wanted God to reveal Himself to me and bring about a new life…I just didn't know how to connect the dots.

Many times we look at the things that are coming out of a person's life and immediately want to judge them based on that evidence. Those who are doing good things, we in turn deem them to be good people; and those who are doing bad, we apply the same rule of thumb. If someone had judged me solely on the evidence of my actions, they would have surely deemed me to be a lost cause. I find great encouragement in the verse found at 1 Samuel 16:7, "But the LORD said to Samuel, 'Do not consider his appearance or his height, for I have rejected him. The LORD does not look at the things people look at. People look at the outward appearance, but the LORD looks at the heart.'"[6]

Now, I am not saying that I was by any stretch of the imagination a great person in action, but what I do know to be true is that there was a longing in my heart that my way of life was not able to fulfill. It didn't matter how much I gave myself to sin, emptiness and hopelessness are all that my efforts were able to achieve. I am not saying that you cannot ever legitimize considering a

[6] 1 Sam. 16:7 (NIV)

person to be a certain thing by the way their life expresses itself in actions. There are situations where that is applicable for sure. All I am saying is that for me this was not the case. I surely did not feel qualified to be received by Jesus in that moment.

A beautiful fact is that God doesn't have to wait in order for you to get yourself together before He is willing to make His way to you. If you had to wait until you were able to get yourself together, you wouldn't ever need Jesus. If you had the power to right all of the wrongs in your life, if you were really able to give yourself the freedom that you so desperately need, if you could produce inner peace, you wouldn't have any need for Jesus; you would be your own God. So then what sense does it make for Jesus to reach out to those that are broken in their sin? Why would that be? First Corinthians tells us:

> Brothers, think of what you were when you were called. Not many of you were wise by human standards; not many of you were influential; not many of you were of noble birth. But God chose the foolish things of the world to shame the wise; God chose the weak things of the world to shame the strong. He chose the lowly things of this world and the despised things—and the things that are not—to nullify the things that are, so that no one may boast before Him. It is because of Him that you

are in Christ Jesus, who has become for us wisdom
from God—that is, our righteousness, holiness and
redemption. Therefore, as it is written: "Let him
who boasts boast in the Lord."[7]

I believe God loves to enlist those considered to be
unlikely suspects into His great story of the unfolding
Kingdom of God and redemption of mankind. God
loves to take lives that the world writes off or those who
feel they would never be able to accomplish anything of
any worth and do the ridiculously impossible with them!
This means you! This definitely means me!

In the Bible in Judges chapter 6 we encounter a man
by the name of Gideon. Without going into all of the
details of the story, I will give you a CliffsNotes version
of what is happening here. Gideon has tucked himself
away in a winepress because an enemy in the Midianites is
ravaging his people, the children of Israel. The Midianites
were overwhelming them and robbing and devouring
them as a people. Gideon has hidden himself away and
is threshing wheat when the angel of the Lord comes to
him there. Upon greeting Gideon he says something that
should be very shocking due to the present circumstances
that Gideon finds himself. He says, "The Lord is with you,
mighty warrior."[8] At this kind of greeting, even Gideon

---

[7] 1 Cor. 1:26-31
[8] Judg. 6:12

is greatly shocked! Gideon begins to present a bunch of excuses and reasons why it is apparent that God is not with the children of Israel, much less with him as an individual. Yet this is what I find to be the beautiful thing about this story: Gideon continues to present issues; God issues identity.

The Angel of the Lord never once engages Gideon on any of the terms that he is throwing out as to why God has not been around or been faithful to them as a people. The Angel of the Lord does not even acknowledge any of the things that Gideon is presenting. In fact, The Lord says this, "Go in the strength you have and save Israel out of the hand of Midian's hand. Am I not sending you?"[9] Gideon continues with factual reasons as to why God should not be able to use him; his clan is the weakest in Manasseh and he is the least in all of his family. At this The Lord says simply, "I will be with you, and you will strike down all the Midianites, leaving none alive."[10]

Gideon was in complete unbelief that God could and would want to use him. There were many circumstantial things against him, in his mind, as to why he should not have been a worthy nominee for such a valiant role, yet God chose him. This is the extraordinary part of the story: God came looking for him. Gideon had isolated

---

[9] Judg. 6:14
[10] Judg. 6:15-16

himself in a place and behavior that didn't quite match up to who God said he was, and yet God saw in him what he didn't even see in himself.

He was hiding; God called him out. He wasn't a part of the fight, yet God called him a mighty warrior. He was alone and felt God had abandoned them. God told him to go in the strength he had and that He would be with him to victory. Wow! How many times do we allow our self-appraisal to limit what we attempt in life? Like Gideon, we too have a lot of circumstantial evidence as to why God shouldn't be able to or wouldn't want to use us to do something significant.

How many times do we allow our self-appraisal to limit what we attempt in life?

Maybe you, like Gideon, have tucked yourself away in a behavior that is not in alignment with who and what God says you are. Maybe you have been hiding in this place as a way to cope with all of the excuses that you have as to why you have legitimately put yourself in this place. We don't read of anybody forcing Gideon into the winepress, which tells me that he was willingly hiding in this place. Have you willingly tucked yourself away? Have you continued to focus more on the issues of life that constantly stare you down rather than on the great identity that God is speaking life into? Gideon presented issues; God issued identity.

This is not a story of what to do and what not to do. Once you realize who you really are, you won't be able to do anything but what you are supposed to do! We have to stop putting limitations on our life by all of the factors around us that we feel are boundaries or argu-

There is no place too far, no issue too great, that God cannot come to you there to free you and release you into purpose!

ments for living a life of defeat. You must find out what God says about you. You must align your life with this truth. There is no place too far, no issue too great, that God cannot come to you there to free you and release you into purpose!

I had to fully realize that before I ever even knew what a desire to love Jesus or pursue Him was all about, that He was pursuing me! We are only able to pursue Him because He has first decided to pursue us! This is a truth that we need to grasp, regardless of how hard it may be to realize. Jesus is pursuing me? Without a doubt He is. The Bible is not man's quest to find God; it is God's story of His pursuit of man. God wholeheartedly pursues you. God wants to break into the life that you live and encounter you, and He will go to great lengths in order to do this.

God is not just satisfied with study about Him. He wants you to encounter Him and to come to really know

Him. Study without encounter will leave you hollow. Experience of what we study is what gives us substance. Experiencing God is what satisfies the souls of men. Experiencing God is what fulfills the longing desires of our hearts. Experiencing God is what ruins us for the passions and pleasures of this world. Religion teaches a system or a process by which man can attempt to make himself right before God. I was not in need of a good system. I did not need someone to walk me through a good behavioral process. I needed someone to walk me to the presence of Jesus. We must experience Him!

God is undoubtedly more than willing to meet you wåhere you are and encounter you in such a way that would leave you changed for the rest of your days.

God encountered Moses in front of a burning bush. Jacob had a wrestling match that lasted all night long with an angel. The woman of Samaria bumped into Jesus by the well and was never the same. Paul was thrown from his horse on the road to Damascus while carrying out what he thought was God's will for his life. God is undoubtedly more than willing to meet you where you are and encounter you in such a way that would leave you changed for the rest of your days. Is this the God that you think about whenever you consider what He could be like? Or do you have a picture of a cold, calloused, condemning God that sits out in the world of the abstract somewhere and just waits for an opportunity to pour out His anger and wrath on you for the times that you have fallen short? My idea of God, if I had one at all, would have definitely been the second of the two. Say this out loud to yourself, "I am being pursued by God." How did that feel? Whatever the feeling, it is truer than you may be willing to accept. He died for you. He longs for you. He is pursuing you.

Before we can ever talk about trusting God and pursuing whatever He may have put in your heart, you must be settled in the fact that God desires you with a love so intense that it could never be matched by anyone or anything. God is pursuing you right now and longing for the moment that you will encounter Him and be overtaken by His goodness and His love. We must live from this place. Our hearts must come to be fully satisfied by Him before we make a move toward anything else.

What is it that God has placed in your heart? What excites you when you begin to enter into it in your thoughts? What is in your heart that causes you to become passionate about life? Is it going back to finish the degree, or attempting it for the first time? Is it stepping out and starting that business? Is it the launch of a ministry? Is it the thought of taking the first steps toward repairing the broken pieces of relationships around you? Is it the restoring of your family that has fallen apart? Whatever it is, one thing I know for sure is that the Father is more excited about seeing you fulfill your purpose than you may be!

If we cannot see God correctly, we will see ourselves incompletely. When we see ourselves incompletely, we will disqualify ourselves from living the life that we see in our heart and desire to make a reality. What is waiting for you upon the water top of life that you have already disqualified yourself for? Is it that everyone in your life has written you off and doesn't think you have the potential or the value in order to accomplish something great? Are you under the influence of words that people have spoken to you all your life that have now shaped the reality you live in?

At times in life you may not have very much control over your starting point, but you can definitely choose how you are going to finish! You may not be able to see all of the steps outlined before you as to how it is going to come to pass. You may not have been given a complete blueprint from the Lord as to when and where it will all come together. But the one thing you can do is make the decision today to penetrate the edge of the boat and put your foot on the surface of the water. Can you hear it now? "Come!"

3

Identity Issues

John 1:12

> "Yet to all who received him, to those who believed in his name, he gave the right to become children of God."

Last chapter we spent time qualifying that God delights in encountering the unlikely candidate and enlisting them into His great unfolding love story to redeem humankind. For some, the challenge isn't so much the way that others around us see us; it is the way that we view ourselves. Self-perception affects everything that we do in life. The way we see ourselves has serious implications on the opportunities that we qualify ourselves for and those that we immediately disqualify ourselves for. It is all based on the condition of who we feel we are.

What do you base this internal opinion off of? Is it the things that your parents have told you all of your life? Is it completely based off of your performance at work and the identity that you have created for yourself in the office amongst your coworkers? Is it by the degree/degrees that you have acquired? Do you identify yourself by a long list of mistakes and things that you believe have gone wrong in life? What is the determining factor for the way that you see yourself? Whether you realize it or not, your own self-appraisal is contributing a great deal to the life that you are either living fulfilled, or unfulfilled.

The issue of identity is one that many face. Many go their entire life attempting to create a place for themselves in the world, never really being at peace with knowing who they truly are and what they are all about. What I mean is this: If you were to have it all taken away, who would you be? If you removed the friends, the ministry responsibility, the career, the titles, the degrees, the plaques, the space that you have created for yourself in the realm of work, who are you? Are you completely defined by the things that you have done or the role that you are fulfilling right now? Are you really nothing more than just a sum total of accomplishments…issues?

The way that we see ourselves is key to trusting God. If I don't see Him correctly, then I cannot see myself completely. A distorted view of God gives me an incomplete view of who I really am. In order to see myself completely, I must see Him correctly. If I don't see Him correctly, I will always question His ways. If I can't see Him correctly, I will always lack the ability to fully believe what He speaks. Not seeing Him correctly leaves me in a place where I cannot fully obey because I cannot fully trust that He may have my best interests at heart. If I don't see Him correctly I will always feel that I have the need of adding to or taking away from what it is that He says to me in order to feel secure.

John tells us that all those who believe are given the right to be the children of God.[11] Children are sons and daughters. Some time ago, The Lord asked me, "Mike, are you satisfied being a son?" To be honest, I was very hesitant to respond. I know that when the Lord asks you a question, it is not because He is unaware of the answer. It is not that God Himself is asking me a question so that I can fill Him in on the information that He is lacking and needs me to clue Him in on. So I answered in the only way that seemed right in the moment and said, "Of course I am, Lord…."

---

[11] John 1:12 (NIV)

This was the beginning of a process of unraveling that began in my life that is still having radical implications as to the way I walk out my life with Him. It is not all right for us to just know the right answer and respond that way if we truly don't believe it ourselves; the process in front of us will always prove empty confession. The Lord, in His great love for us, will walk us through processes and places in life in order to reveal to us the shallow, or incomplete, places in our confession or life. This was the beginning of a lesson on identity, and that identity being one of a son.

Sonship is something that you do not hear a lot about. I came to find out that I had not been living my life from the place of a son. In fact, I found out that I had been living my life with God from the position and with the perspective of a slave. The differences between the two have completely changed my life. Motive makes all the difference in the world. We can be in the right behavior with the wrong drive in our heart. We can be found doing all of the right things and still not be the right thing ourselves.

The book of Exodus tells the story of the children of Israel and their deliverance out of Egypt. Joseph dies at the end of Genesis and prophesies that God will come to their aid and will bring them out of the land of Egypt and into the land that He had sworn to their forefather

Abraham. They were working as slaves in the nation of Egypt under the rule of King Pharaoh for a period of just about four hundred years. This means that there were several generations that lived and died under the conditions of a slave. For several hundreds of years, slavery was the only lens of life that eyes were able to engage the world by. The life of a slave was all that they knew. Day after day they were working to please a pagan king. Then the Lord raises up Moses in order to be the catalyst in a miraculous series of events that ends with their deliverance out of Egyptian captivity. Once freed, they find themselves out in the wilderness having to learn what it means to walk with God. The issue many times is not finding freedom; it is finding stability and consistency in being free.

The issue many times is not finding freedom; it is finding stability and consistency in being free.

The issue of identity begins to unfold immediately after they are freed from slavery. Once on the other side of the sea and the waters are closing in on Pharaoh and his army, if we look close enough at what takes place, we will see the issue of a people who were unwilling to occupy the place of a son. It had only been three days and already the children of Israel began to grumble and complain about their circumstances and the way they felt

God was treating them. The first issue that comes to the surface is over the perceived problem of not having any water in Exodus chapter 15. God brings them to Mara, but they cannot drink the water because it is bitter, and so the grumbling begins. Because of this, Moses cries out to God and God shows him a piece of wood. Moses throws the piece of wood into the waters and the waters instantly become sweet. Problem solved, or not.[12]

The beginning of chapter 16 tells us that it was about forty days later, and, once again, the children of Israel were bickering and complaining. This time the issue was not about having any water for them to drink; this time the present issue was about not having any meat to their liking. This was their confession of faith in the moment, "If only we had died by the Lord's hand in Egypt! There we sat around pots of meat and ate all the food we wanted, but you have brought us out into this desert to starve this entire assembly to death."[13] At this point, this seems a little ridiculous to believe. After all that they saw the Lord do for them, they have the nerve to complain about the menu options once God comes to the rescue? Are they serious? Yes, they are very serious.

The beginning of Exodus chapter 17 is no different from the last two. Once again the children of Israel

---

[12] Ex. 15:22-25 (NIV)
[13] Ex. 16:3.

encounter an issue where there doesn't seem to be any water, and they begin to grumble against their leader, Moses, again. Verse 3 of chapter 17 says, "But the people were thirsty for water there, and they grumbled against Moses. They said, "Why did you bring us up out of Egypt to make us and our children and livestock die of thirst?" Again Moses cried out to God, and God answers with a miracle of provision. Moses goes on ahead of the people with the staff in his hand and some of the elders of Israel. Then God stands before him at the rock of Horeb and commands Moses to strike the rock and water begins to come out of it for the people.[14] This time for sure the problem had to be solved...right? I mean, come on, once again they tested the intentions of the Lord, and He miraculously provided for them. How many times could we go through this?

The issue at hand is one that goes much deeper than just mere provision of daily necessities. They had lived for many generations as slaves. And whether or not you believe it to be true, your present context of living has a powerful effect on the way you see yourself and the world around you...and even God Himself. As a slave you have to constantly work for your worth, day after day working and slaving over your tasks in order to create a short-lived value for yourself. Even if you had accomplished a

---

[14] Ex. 17:1-7

great amount in a day, there was always going to be more work waiting for you tomorrow. Slaves are accustomed to working to prove themselves. Working for their worth was a way of life for the children of Israel for a very long time—almost four hundred years...remember?

Just living as a slave and having to work for your worth is not the end of the story. Living with the mind-set of a slave means you see the world through the lens of a slave, and this is where we get to the heart of the issue. When you see the world through the lens of a slave, you are given to the principle in life that work equals worth. And when work equals worth, it only makes sense that those who would be able to do more work would be worthy of greater worth. Yet there is a significant complication with this paradigm for life. When you are living and seeing the world around you through the lens of a slave, not only do you have to work in order to prove your worth to those around you, but also those around you have to work in order to prove their worth to you.

This is where the point of contention multiplies. This is why as long as things were going good for the children of Israel and God was showing up with miracles and provision, they were willing to follow and their devotion was strong. However, the moment they walked into a situation where it seemed as if God was not actively working for them, they lost all value of their commitment to God. They were not connected with the ways of the Lord; they only had an attachment to the works of the Lord.

Hebrews 3 tells us, "So, as the Holy Spirit says: 'Today if you hear His voice, do not harden your hearts as you did in the rebellion, during the time of testing in the desert, where your forefathers tested and tried me and for forty years saw what I did. That is why I was angry with that generation, and I said, "Their hearts are always going astray, and they have not known my ways." ' "[15] "They have not known My ways" is what God had to say about them.

What does God have to say about you? Do you know if you are connected to the ways of the Lord? One way to find out a quick answer to that question is to examine your behavior and attitude during the times of life in which it seems as if God is absent from the scene. **How do you handle the seasons where it seems as if heaven is silent and your prayers don't seem to be getting miraculous results?** How do you handle the seasons where it seems as if heaven is silent and your prayers don't seem to be getting miraculous results? This quick check will give you insight as to where you currently stand.

---

[15] Heb. 3:7-10

In order to really be connected to the ways of an individual you have to know them. Just knowing about somebody will not get the job done. We can go through history and study the lives of great men and women that have gone before us in order to come to great conclusions about their lives, but, at best, it would just be a collection of information about a person. You see, in order to really connect with the people of the past, we would have had to have been alive in their day in order to walk alongside them and interact with them. A collection of information or data about a given individual will not connect you with their heart.

If we are not connected with the ways of the Lord, we will always second-guess our commitment to Him when walking through situations that we don't like, or wouldn't have chosen for ourselves. If we don't know the heart of God toward us, we will walk through the wilderness seasons of life and question, just like the children of Israel, why God is attempting to kill us. When God doesn't seem to be working for us, we will question His love for us. When God is not performing miracles in front of our eyes at our every request, we will wonder why He has abandoned us and left us to die. The children of Israel were dealing with an issue of identity; they might have lived under the conditions of a slave for quite some time and saw themselves in that light, but that is not what God saw.

God did not come and redeem Israel from Egypt as just mere slaves; He redeemed them as sons and daughters. This change in perspective makes all the difference. Israel was already the right thing in the eyes of the Lord. They just couldn't rid themselves of a slave mentality in order to trust God and enter into the promise of the Promised Land. They had received the word from God about wanting to bring them into a land flowing with milk and honey and obviously saw that God was powerful enough to make good on that promise, but a self-perception issue plagued them and ultimately infected them to where they missed out on all that God had wanted to do for them. The inheritance was never promised, nor will it ever be given, to a slave. The inheritance has always and will always be granted to a son.

We don't live in the days where a son grows up working alongside his father in hopes of one day having Dad deem him to be the right man for the inheritance to be given. We don't have the same processes as generations before us where sons would joyfully anticipate the day that Dad will look them in the eye and declare them "a man" ready for the task. This has great significance and even extreme importance to the way we view the ways of the Lord.

A son grows up his whole life knowing that one day Dad is going to pass on to him the inheritance that is due to him as a son. With this being the case, a son doesn't have to view the processes and disciplines of the Father as something that is damaging or threatening to the inheritance due him. Any discipline or time in the wilderness is no longer something that is to punish me; rather, it is in place to perfect me!

When you know that Daddy already has something with your name on it, because you are his son, which means you are the right thing from the beginning, you don't have to fight and strive in order to keep your inheritance in place. All you have to do is continue to follow in line with the things that Dad puts in front of you because you know that He has your best interest at heart in developing you for what He has for you. So the issue is not one of punishment, but perfection. You are being perfected for the place of promise. The wilderness is a place where the Father can strengthen you before bringing you into what He has for you. The wilderness is a place where you can grow into what the Father wants to give to you.

The wilderness is a place where the Father can strengthen you before bringing you into what He has for you.

Sons don't have to fight and strive for the acceptance of their father; they are born into a place that deems them worthy of everything their father has. This is the case with the children of God. Once you are born again, you don't have to fight for acceptance. You don't have to grumble and quarrel for worth and value. You are already the right thing. You are a son and a daughter. There is no greater title to be given. In moving through the processes of the Lord, you don't have to work *for* a place of value, but rather you work *from* a place of value.

Slaves work to prove their value *to* others; sons work to produce value *in* others. So many of us come to know Jesus and then attempt to strive to prove ourselves worthy enough to walk with Him. And by doing so, the motive behind the actions that we undertake, rather than being compelled from a place of love and sincere acceptance, is from where we press to prove to those around us, ourselves, and even God Himself that we are worthy enough for the things He has called us to.

This fleshly striving will never enable us to occupy the place of promise. It would be far from the truth to say that hard work and diligence do not have their place for those living in the Kingdom. What I am saying is that you will never be able, by works, to prove your way into the promise/inheritance of God. The inheritance is something that can only be given. It is a gift. Like salvation will never be by works; it is a gift.

There is great peace that comes from knowing that I can trust the Father to place me into what He has for me when the time is right. I don't have to attempt to outdo anybody when I know that there is a place for me.

There is great peace that comes from knowing that I can trust the Father to place me into what He has for me when the time is right.

I don't have to try to impress others around me in order to manipulate my way into the place. I can trust His ways. There is no need for me to continue to look at people as the gateway into the promise. I can keep my eyes on the Father knowing that when the time is right, He is going to move all the people and places necessary in order to grant me the inheritance He has promised me.

The kingdom of this world says that the harder you work, the more you are worth. The more you do, the more you deserve. This seems to be at odds with the Kingdom of God where we have received the very best of heaven while we were yet at our worst. In a time when we were yet afar off, Jesus came and died for us.[16] There seem to be different principles at work here in determining our value as sons. Which side of the coin do you find yourself living by? There is great peace and freedom on the side of the son, living out of a place. There is great unrest and striving on the side of the slave, living to earn a place.

---

[16] Rom. 5:8 (NIV)

The issue with the mentality of a slave versus a son seems to be one that the children of Israel had a hard time identifying…but what about you? I didn't think this would apply to me in the way that the Lord revealed to me. In the days that I was not walking with the Lord, and was at my very worst, there would be months that I would go without talking with my earthly father. In fact, us talking usually stemmed from me being arrested or in a serious amount of trouble. When we would talk, he would typically ask, "What did you do now, Mike?" Well, this question being asked by my father was sown deep within my heart. I came into a place of feeling that the only time we could talk was if I had done something wrong. I felt the only way in order to receive the attention of my father was for me to do something for it. After coming to know the Lord, this question still sat within my heart, "What did you do, Mike?"

My view of my earthly father had great implications on the way that I viewed the Lord, and so I began to work. Without ever knowing that in my heart was this deep-rooted issue of having to perform my way into the good graces of the Father, I worked. I did a lot of great things. I was able to impact lives and press toward things that, in and of themselves, were really good things, but the motivating factor of my heart was one that felt if I could just do enough, God would favor me. If I could just do enough, I could better my position with the Father. If I could just do enough, God would continue to keep open lines of communication with me.

I held the mentality of a slave while in the position of a son. I was attempting to work my way into the things that the Father wanted to give freely to me all along. When I wasn't doing, I felt as if I wasn't worthy of the Father's attention or affection because I had nothing to present to Him in order to make me worthy. A small and seemingly insignificant situation with my earthly father had major effects on how I was living my life, and this is after I was already saved and walking with God.

Many times we don't think about the way that these types of situations impact us. Maybe it wasn't that your dad always asked you the same question that I was being asked whenever I found myself to be in great amounts of trouble. Maybe your situation was/is completely different than mine. Maybe your father or mother always spoke negatively to you and limited you as an individual with the things you felt capable of doing, and now you have a hard time believing that God could want to make something great out of your life. Maybe you had an abusive parent and now you have a hard time connecting with the reality that God is a gracious and loving Father. Maybe you had a parent that you never knew or you grew up never having ever connected with your earthly parents, and it has now left this deep wound within you.

The possibilities are endless, but the reality is that we must be able to come to the place where we identify these perspectives for what they are—and that is false realities. God's desire is for this to be broken in your life. He wants to heal and restore you so that you may see Him correctly and live out your life in fullness and with great joy.

How many of us fall into this rut? How easy is it to be birthed into the Kingdom of God and yet still have the principles of the world operating in us and through us? A performance-based mentality is what someone would typically call this type of living that I was engaged in. What I had to come to realize is that it will never be by *worth* that I was brought into the Kingdom, but by *birth*. Jesus told Nicodemus that unless a man is born again he would not be able to see the Kingdom of God.[17]

We are in the Kingdom by birth. We have been positioned in this life for such a time as this by birth. We were born into this! We have been born again into a position that makes us worthy, makes us valuable, and makes us partakers of God's best because of our faith in Jesus!

We have to connect with the Father in a deeper place than just what He is able to do for us. Yes, all of the doing that God does is great and awesome, yet all of the doing is just a sign to His being. The miracles of God have always

---

[17] John 3:3 (NIV)

been a doorway to bring us into the character and the heart of God. God does because of who He is. He is not to be defined by the things that He does, but rather the things that He does just gives the expression of who He is! Returning to the verses in Hebrews 3, God says, "… where your fathers tested Me, tried Me, and saw My works for forty years." They saw the works of the Lord for forty years, and yet somehow never moved past the works to connect with His ways.

Have you allowed the works of the Lord to connect you with the ways of the Lord? Are you living your life with God just surviving from one miracle to the next? God wants you to connect with His heart. We have to be willing to look past the *hands* of God in order to see the *heart* of God. Only then will our lives escape the need for God to perform for us in order to prove His love for us. God wants to establish you in deep and consistent places of intimacy. Intimacy produces confidence. Confidence enables freedom. Freedom allows you to see God correctly and yourself completely!

We have to be willing to look past the *hands* of God in order to see the *heart* of God.

Your intimacy with God isn't supposed to be determined by your perspective of your current circumstances, but rather, intimacy is to be determined by the great revelation of the heart of God toward you. Pray that God would reveal His heart to you and that you would truly pursue to establish consistent intimacy with Him out of this place.

4

Intimacy Denied

God has always desired to be intimately connected to His people. Even back in the Old Testament we can see God desiring intimacy with His people. In chapter 19 of Exodus we find that God is ready to make a move that would radically change the relationship He had with the children of Israel. For the most part, any communication that God had with the children of Israel had come through Moses. In an effort to increase the level of intimacy and personal contact that God had with the children of Israel, He gave certain instructions to Moses for them:

> In the third month after the Israelites left Egypt—
> on the very day—they came to the Desert of
> Sinai. After they set out from Rephidim, they

entered the Desert of Sinai, and Israel camped there in the desert in front of the mountain. Then Moses went up to God, and the Lord called to him from the mountain and said, "This is what you are to say to the house of Jacob and what you are to tell the people of Israel: 'You yourselves have seen what I did to Egypt, and how I carried you on eagles' wings and brought you to myself. Now if you obey me fully and keep my covenant, then out of all nations you will be my treasured possession. Although the whole earth is mine, you will be for me a kingdom of priests and a holy nation.' These are the words you are to speak to the Israelites."[18]

This is a pivotal moment in the story. God is now leading them to the place beyond the miracles, into intimacy and relationship. The miracles were great in that they provided for the children of Israel a way out of Egypt, but God was not only interested in bringing them out... His plan the whole time was to bring them to Himself. The miracles were a sign, a doorway, an opening for them to be able to find the purpose of God the whole way through, which was and will always be deep intimate relationship and revelation. God could have rescued them and then let them be once they had made their way clear

---

[18] Ex. 19:1-6

away from Pharaoh. God could have just told Moses to tell the people, "Just remember Me every once in a while and we will call it even; just don't ever forget who did this for you." But that is not the ways of God. The works of God will always, if we are willing to see beyond the miracle in front of us, lead us to the ways of God…every time. Miracles help me to see the miracle worker. We were never intended to become satisfied with the miracles in and of themselves.

Let's continue with the story to see the response of Moses and the children of Israel. You would think after all of this, that they would surely get it by now.

So Moses went back and summoned the elders of the people and set before them all the words the Lord had commanded him to speak. The people all responded together, "We will do everything the Lord has said." So Moses brought their answer back to the Lord.

The Lord said to Moses, "I am going to come to you in a dense cloud, so that the people will hear me speaking with you and will always put their trust in you." Then Moses told the Lord what the people had said.

And the Lord said to Moses, "Go to the people and consecrate them today and tomorrow. Have them wash their clothes and be ready by the third day, because on that day the Lord will come down on Mount Sinai in the sight of all the people. Put limits for the people around the mountain and tell them, 'Be careful that you do not go up the mountain or touch the foot of it. Whoever touches the mountain shall surely be put to death. He shall surely be stoned or shot with arrows; not a hand is to be laid on him. Whether man or animal, he shall not be permitted to live....'"

After Moses had gone down the mountain to the people, he consecrated them, and they washed their clothes. Then he said to the people, "Prepare yourselves for the third day. Abstain from sexual relations."

On the morning of the third day there was thunder and lightning, with a thick cloud over the mountain, and a very loud trumpet blast. Everyone in the camp trembled. Then Moses led the people out of the camp to meet with God, and they stood at the foot of the mountain. Mount Sinai was covered with smoke, because the Lord descended on it in fire. The smoke billowed up from it like smoke from a furnace, the whole mountain trembled violently, and the sound of the trumpet grew louder and louder. Then Moses spoke and the voice of God answered him. [19]

Let's, for a moment, assess the situation at hand. Moses has gone to the mountain to meet with God. God has revealed to Moses that He is ready to connect with the people in a way that has been absent up until this moment. Moses is to go back to the people and inform them of the intentions of the Lord and prepare them for this glorious fulfillment where God will meet with them and they will each be able to have a personal relationship with Him directly. God is ready to eliminate the middleman, being Moses, and engage the children of Israel directly. God desires relationship.

This seems to be a beautiful strategy on God's behalf, and who wouldn't want to know God directly? The thought of having been enslaved and held in captivity for so long only then to be rescued by the Creator of all things and now to be able to not just know *of* Him but to know *Him*! The children of Israel must have been absolutely enthralled at the thought of meeting with God! I imagine those must have been three very long days filled with much talk and excitement over the opportunity that stood before them. A door was opened up to them bigger than anything they had ever known. Surely they

---

[19] Ex. 19:7-19

would accept and humbly come to meet with God. They responded accordingly to Moses, "We will do everything the Lord has said."[20]

What we find is that after Moses comes back down the mountain from meeting with God, the tune of the Israelites had shifted once again. When the people saw the thunder and lightning and heard the trumpet and saw the mountain in smoke, they trembled with fear. *They stayed at a distance* and said to Moses, "Speak to us yourself and we will listen. But do not have God speak to us or we will die."[21] The children of Israel, in fear, decided that they would rather just continue to deal with Moses, the middleman, and not come to connect with God directly. This seems to be the mentality of a slave once again surfacing in their life in the most inopportune of moments.

We have already come to the conclusion that the children of Israel spent a period of about four hundred years living in Egyptian slavery. During that time they would have been accustomed to a taskmaster or a slave driver. A taskmaster would have been the one to daily receive orders from Pharaoh as to what they were to be working on for that day. Daily the taskmaster would receive instructions from Pharaoh and drive the Israelites through their daily laborious activities. Does this start to sound familiar at all?

---

[20] Ex. 19:8
[21] Ex. 20:18-19 (NIV)

Sometimes it is the very thing that we want to abandon that we can't seem to get away from. Although not wanting to live under slave-like conditions, it was all that they knew, all that they had experienced.

In a moment of panic and fear, they resorted to the thing that came natural for them and that was to deal with Moses directly and let God speak to Moses. In this equation God would take the place of Pharaoh, and Moses would take the place of the taskmaster, and they would still be able to live in perceived freedom and familiarity. Rather than connecting with God and coming into the new reality of relationship that God desired, they stayed captive to a mind-set that, although they were free on the outside, they were still in captivity in their minds to an old paradigm of life.

What could it be that God truly desires to bring you into, but you can't get out of thought processes that continue to be a setback for you?

Sometimes it is not the things that we need to learn that become the most difficult task in our walk of faith, but rather it is the ways of life and the thought processes of the past that we can't unlearn that still plague us and seek to be our downfall. They could not abandon old ways of thinking in order to enter into new realities with

God. What is it about your way of thinking that could be limiting you right now from walking in new realities with God? What could it be that God truly desires to bring you into, but you can't get out of thought processes that continue to be a setback for you? Is there anything about your old way of life or environments of the past that continue to want to attach themselves to you and find themselves surfacing in your life in the most inopportune of moments?

Every time it looks like you are going to get a break-through, here come those thoughts of negativity again. Every time it seems as if your life is going to be full of joy and peace, here come those thoughts of depression again. Every time it seems as if you are going to be able to step out and grab hold of new opportunities in life, here come those thoughts of unworthiness again. What is it about your thought life that needs to be addressed in order to move forward with the Lord? The children of Israel were held back that day because, even though they found them-selves in a new place, they did not have a renewed mind. Romans chapter 12 tells us that we can be transformed by the renewing of our mind.[22]

A renewed mind is what makes all the difference if we are truly to be changed. Many will say that if they

---

[22] Rom. 12:2 (NIV)

can just find themselves in a different environment, things will change for them. If you can just find yourself in a different financial situation, then things will be different. If you can just find your way into a new situation, then you will have what you need in order to become a new person. This may be true in the slightest of chances, but in reality, the real change that needs to take place is within your thinking; your mind must be renewed.

The issue is not really the people around you; it is not the condition of your finances; and it is not necessarily the environment where you find yourself; it is the issue of a renewed mind. Plenty will change all of the variables around them and

Our mind must be renewed if we are going to continue to move forward into the new things that God wants to do.

somehow find their way back into the same set of circumstances, just with new faces and places. We must come to realize that until we renew our minds, what is in our heart will always find its way to us. We won't have to look that hard. We won't have to go that far. What we desire from within us will always find its ways to us. Proverbs tell us that as a man thinks in his heart, so is he.[23]

---

[23] Prov. 23:7 (NIV)

Jacob was a man that had lived his life in a home where there was deception and evil practice; his very name means "deceiver." Yet for some reason, as you follow the life of Jacob, it didn't matter where he was, the same things always surfaced…deception. He and his mom deceived his father in order to rob his brother, Esau, of the promised birthright. He found himself fleeing and going to his uncle Laban's house, and deception seems to find him there yet again.

We can continue to move the people and the places in our life continually if that's the way we want to go about it, but eventually after there are no more people and places to move and no more blame to push around, we will have to come and confront the truth…that it was us the entire time. We must have a renewed mind. Our mind must be renewed if we are going to continue to move forward into the new things that God wants to do. A renewed mind is the doorway to transformation. You can find yourself in a new circumstance with an unrenewed mind and still produce old outcomes. It is of dire importance that we pursue a renewed mind!

The children of Israel found themselves out in the desert with God and unable to abandon their old ways of thinking. Because they were unable to abandon their old ways of thinking, they purposefully denied themselves the intimacy that God wanted to establish with them individually. They proclaimed, "God, You speak to Moses, and we will deal with him." How many of us today deny ourselves the intimacy that God wants to establish with us because we are unable to move past the middleman and connect with God directly?

Maybe you have a relationship with a great church. Maybe you have a phenomenal pastor that speaks to you and into you weekly. Maybe you have surrounded yourself with the best of people pursuing God that you can find. But in the midst of all of that, what does your connection with God look like? What kind of life and vibrancy does it have? Have you made the decision in your heart to chase God up the mountain and establish the intimacy He so desires and has made available? Or are you standing like the children of Israel at the foot of the mountain in fear and resisting the very thing that God wants to do?

God wants you to move past His hands and the things that He may do in order for you to be deeply rooted in His heart and who He is.

You are desired. Intimacy with God is there for the taking. We are responsible for the level of intimacy that we have with God. That may sound harsh, but it is true. You can't get out what you are not willing to invest. That is the way that it works in any relationship. Why would this be perceived to be different? It's not. God is waiting. God wants to establish you in consistent places of intimacy. God wants you to move past His hands and the things that He may do in order for you to be deeply rooted in His heart and who He is. Don't allow the works of the Lord to hinder you from moving on to capturing the ways of the Lord in your life.

5

Satisfaction in God

Satisfaction: 1. An act of satisfying; fulfillment; gratification.

2. The state of being satisfied; contentment.

3. The cause or means of being satisfied.

Psalm 37:4

"Delight yourself in the Lord; And He will give you the desires of your heart."

It is important that we connect with the ways of the Lord so that when we find ourselves experiencing an outcome that we didn't expect, or out in the middle of the wilderness with nothing but a promise, we won't freak out and want to head back to captivity thinking that God has abandoned us or is trying to kill us. Identifying and connecting with the ways of the Lord will preserve us in these wilderness moments. If we have not yet identified God's ways, we will question every wilderness-type experience in our life and qualify it to be something that is against us.

The promise ushers you into the wilderness; this is the way of God. The word of the Lord, most times, will bring you into the wilderness. You will not always go directly from the promise to the palace. You will not always receive the word and then arrive. The wilderness is installed in your life as a way to test what is really in you. Now, take note, the wilderness is not to test to see if you are the right thing. We have already qualified that you *are* the right thing. The wilderness is put in place in your life to see if you are ready. The wilderness tests the satisfactions of the heart.

The wilderness is installed in your life as a way to test what is really in you.

Have you found a place of satisfaction in God? Has your heart been deeply satisfied by God and in God alone? This is a key issue in the discussion of trusting God. If we have not been satisfied by Him and with Him, then we will always strive in our lives for something or someone to fill that place. Worship is nothing more and nothing less than satisfying the thirst of your heart. Wherever you are satisfying that thirst is your place of worship.

In 1 Samuel 17 we read a familiar account about David and Goliath. However, I would like for you to approach the story without all of the preconceived ideas that you already may have about it. In the beginning of 1 Samuel chapter 16, we are told that the prophet Samuel is instructed by God to go and anoint the next king of Israel. God sends the prophet to the house of Jesse in Bethlehem.[24] Upon arriving, Samuel finds that Jesse has eight sons. Although there are eight sons total, only seven are invited to the time of sacrifice with the prophet; David is left out in the field tending to the sheep. After Samuel allows seven of Jesse's sons to pass by in front of him, the Lord instructs him that surely none of them are to be the next king.

After telling Jesse that none had been chosen, Jesse says, "There is still the youngest, but he is out tending to the sheep." Samuel's reply is that, "We will not sit down until he arrives." When David is sent for and enters the room, Samuel anoints him as the next king of Israel. Verse 13 tells us, "So Samuel took the horn of oil and anointed him in the presence of his brothers, and from that day on the Spirit of the LORD came powerfully upon David."[25]

---

[24] 1 Sam. 16:1
[25] 1 Sam. 16:13

This seems to be an interesting position taken by David's father. Jesse blatantly leaves David out in the field tending to the sheep and does not even allow him to come to the ceremony with the prophet Samuel. This must have been devastating to young David. Did David even know that something significant was happening in his home that day? Did he know that he was being left out of the equation and sent out to the field as all the rest of his brothers prepared for the possibility of being anointed? Was it because he was too young? Could it have been because Jesse didn't see enough value in David for him to have been considered for the position of king of Israel? Were David's brothers so much more superiorly talented and qualified for the opportunity that was before them that it warranted subtracting David from the equation?

We don't clearly understand why David was left out in the field with the sheep, but nevertheless, he was left out of the moment. He didn't get an invite to the show. The curtain was about to be drawn back to unveil the next king and nobody had saved David a seat. He didn't even get to peek in the window to watch it all as it unfolded.

There is something great about this scenario that we need to grasp. What is great about this scenario is that even though men left David out, God included him. God knew right where to find David when He needed him. God knew that when the time was right, He would send the prophet to connect with David and anoint him as the next king of Israel. David didn't have to push his way into the conversation. David didn't have to attempt to persuade his dad that he was a better fit for what was happening than his other brothers. David just continued in faithfulness with what was put in front of him. David found a place of worship out in the field. To all of those surrounding David, it didn't seem like much of a task, and that was okay. David learned to worship there in *that* place.

Have you learned to worship in *that* place? Have you developed the ability to worship in the place that doesn't really seem that important? Have you conditioned your heart to worship God even while all those around you may write you off and send you out into the field? David found a place of worship in the field while being left out because his satisfaction wasn't attached to an opportunity. David was able to continue to be faithful and find a place of worship out in the field because his satisfaction wasn't dependent upon having a title. David didn't need anything or anyone to complete him because God had already satisfied him.

Have you allowed your heart to be satisfied by God in the field of life where He may have you now? Or are you one that continually tells yourself, "When I get out of this place, I will start to do…" or, "When I get this responsibility, I will be more passionate…"? Or how about, "When this season of life ends, I will devote myself more." You cannot have these thought processes and think that you have connected with the same place of satisfaction that David found.

You must come to a place in your life where you have connected with the reality that Jesus is all-sufficient for you, all that you need, all that you desire.

The issue of being satisfied is this: You will never submit to supremacy if you first have not found sufficiency. Jesus is more than enough. You must come to a place in your life where you have connected with the reality that Jesus is all-sufficient for you, all that you need, all that you desire. You don't need anything else because He is more than enough. Without this type of passion, we will never truly be able to surrender our hearts to His supremacy.

Why would that be, you ask? If we have not found sufficiency in Jesus, we will continually seek to connect with something in life that will fulfill our hearts. This seeking may express itself in the form of a career choice. It may express itself in the passionate pursuit of having the perfect circle of friends. It could possibly be an issue of social injustice that you are emptying your life into right now. You could be filling this void in your heart with your passion for sports or fitness. It could be the perfect relationship that you have been searching after. But at the end of the day, if Jesus has not first satisfied you, you will not fully submit yourself to His supremacy.

If we are pursuing something or someone harder than we are pursuing Him, we are not truly satisfied. When this is the case, we become unwilling, if asked, to separate ourselves from the person, place, or thing that we have been getting our fill on. If Jesus asks me to walk away from my career because He has something else for me to do…I can't do it. If Jesus asks me to break off the relationship that I've been in because it is not healthy and is becoming a real hindrance in my life…I can't do it. When the Lord attempts to lead me down a path that would mean severing me from my lifeline…I can't do it because I have not been satisfied by Jesus but rather by whatever has been my main pursuit in life.

Jesus is never meant to be a secondary pursuit; nor is the pursuit of Jesus to be used as a means to an end. Many will come to the Lord in hopes that He will do for them what they have always wanted and have not been able to do for themselves. It sounds and looks something like this: I will serve You in hopes that I can get a relationship; I will love You in hopes that You turn my finances around; I will get plugged into church with the expectation that I can get a better job.

Jesus has not, and will not ever be, a platform upon which we stand in order to further pursue our own selfish desires.

This is wrong. Jesus has not, and will not ever be, a platform upon which we stand in order to further pursue our own selfish desires. We must come to a place where we are willing to confront these tendencies within us. We must come to a place where we really begin to identify who we are and what we have been pursuing all along. Some of the things we find out may not be cute and cuddly, and if that's the case, we must put an end to these fleshly initiatives and surrender to the Lord wholeheartedly.

David found satisfaction in the Lord, and it allowed him to be faithful where he was with what was in front of him. What happens after David gets anointed to be the next king of Israel is incredibly important to the story-line here. After the prophet anoints David in front of his family and gives him the word of the Lord that he is to be the next king of Israel, instead of David going and packing his bags so that he can have a royal procession to the palace where he will be enthroned upon high in the sights of the city and all the people, David gets sent back out into the field to continue tending to the sheep. This seems to be wrong. How could this be? Why would God give him a great word such as this and then send him back out into the field? Could this be the way that God operates? Could this be the ways of the Lord? David, similar to the children of Israel years before him, received a word from God that He was going to bring him into something much bigger than him. The children of Israel, upon receiving the word, found themselves brought out into the wilderness. David found himself, upon receiving the word, back out in the field—the wilderness, if you will.

There is something to the way that God will speak to you and then test you. The only way that we are able to find out who and what we are is to be tested. Until we are tested, all we have is a hopeful confession. I can tell you what I would like to do…what I think I would do…what I hope I will do if put in a certain circumstance or handed a certain situation. But until I actually have to confront a certain thing, I really don't know what I am going to do. I really don't know the person that I would be if I found myself in a certain predicament.

> **It is our seasons in the wilderness that gives us a depth that we are unable to attain by any other means.**

It is the time of testing that adds substance to who we are. It is our seasons in the wilderness that gives us a depth that we are unable to attain by any other means. There is a special blessing for those who learn to embrace the wilderness times of life. There are certain revelations that you cannot get anywhere else other than out in the wilderness with God. David was very familiar with the wilderness, and he benefited greatly for it.

The wilderness is not a place to destroy me but rather to develop me. The wilderness is not against me; it is something that God has created for me. The wilderness is where I truly find out what I am all about. The wilderness will reveal to you what you are made of. Hollow confessions are exposed in the wilderness. Fancy quotes and empty catchphrases are brought into the light in the wilderness. The wilderness is a place where you will have to confront what is really of substance in your walk with God and what has been religious fluff all along. The little one-liners and gimmicks won't work out in the wilderness. The formulated prayers that you have memorized that have no life and no passion won't work out in the wilderness.

When you find yourself in the wilderness stripped of everything that you thought you were and removed from all the activity, it is in that place where you face the reality of truly being broken before God. The wilderness is a place where you are stripped of all but God to truly find out if you are satisfied with God and God alone. The wilderness is a place where you are far removed from all of the lifeless religious behaviors in your life that you depend on to hold you up; all of the empty habits that are no longer leading you to touch the Lord, leading you to life.

The Lord must bring us to this place if we are to be used. The Lord must have broken vessels that He can fill to overflowing with Himself. The Lord will not compete with you for whose agenda will prevail. The Lord will not contend with you over whose name is going to be more famous. You must be broken. The wilderness has produced many broken vessels. However, there are many that enter into the wilderness that haven't found a way to embrace that place and so have worked their way out of a divine season of the Lord. We must be willing to surrender. David surrendered. David returned to the field.

The wilderness is a place where you are stripped of all but God to truly find out if you are satisfied with God and God alone.

There is nothing that will kill the pride of a man more than to give him a great vision of tomorrow and then send him off to work in obscurity and hiddenness today. This is where David found himself. David is carrying a vision of becoming king and yet is returning to tend to the sheep out in a place where he is not even recognized. Is this where you find yourself? What do you do when your experiences are not matching your expectations?

God knows that we have it within us to become better by embracing the wilderness seasons of life.

This tension is the greatest purifier of our motives. This tension is what proves to us why we are really involved. This tension will either cause us to be better or to be bitter. God knows that we have it within us to become better by embracing the wilderness seasons of life. The wilderness will add to you. The wilderness will strengthen you. The wilderness will cause you to sift through who you thought you were and connect with what you are really about.

Are you carrying a word for tomorrow and yet find yourself in a place today that doesn't seem to line up? Is your challenge that you can't seem to fit your "right now" into the equation of your "what will be?" I am sure this is where David was. Anointed to be king of Israel and all he is sent to lead is the sheep out in the field of obscurity. David would soon have his moment, and so will you. David would soon find himself in another field of opportunity that would continue to test the satisfaction of his heart. David would prove himself faithful. David would continue to trust God.

WHY GOLIATH?

Some time later David's father, Jesse, would send David to take food to his brothers out on the battlefield where they found themselves engaged in somewhat of a war with the Philistines. First Samuel 17 gives the report that the battle lines had been drawn between the army of the Philistines and the armies of Saul. The Philistines were gathered at Sokoh in Ephes Dammim. Saul and the men of Israel were gathered together and encamped in the Valley of Elah. The Philistines were on one mountain and Israel on a mountain on the other side with nothing but a valley of opportunity between them.[26] This is where David's father sends him.

Upon David arriving and setting down the stuff he had brought for his brothers, the Philistine champion, Goliath, took his routine post that he had taken for the previous forty days, twice a day, in order to taunt the army of Israel. For forty straight days the men of Israel had prepared themselves for battle and gone out to the front lines only to be taunted and embarrassed by Goliath. Goliath questioned them repeatedly in saying, "Why have you come out to line up for battle? Am I not a Philistine, and you the servants of Saul? Choose a man for your-selves, and let him come down to me. If he is able to fight with me and kill me, then we will be your servants. But if I prevail against him and kill him, then you shall be our servants and serve us." And the Philistine said, "I defy the

---

[26] 1 Sam. 17:1-3 (NIV)

armies of Israel this day; give me a man that we may fight together."

This may not have been such an intimidating situation had Goliath been the size of a regular man. But Goliath was a giant. Goliath, according to the Bible, was nine and a half feet tall and had armor that would have been almost impossible to carry by a man of normal size.[27] Goliath was a giant-sized problem for the army of Israel, and the Bible says that they were dismayed and greatly afraid. This is the scene that David walks into.

Something different happens when David walks onto the scene and sees and hears what is happening. Verse 23 of 1 Samuel 17 tells us explicitly that David heard the words of Goliath. And while the men were fleeing from fear, David began to inquire. David asked, "What shall be done for the man who kills this Philistine and takes away the reproach from Israel? For who is this uncircumcised Philistine, that he should defy the armies of the living God?"[28] Right from the onset of the issue David has a different perspective than the rest that are involved. David sees Goliath as a reproach to Israel, yes, but he also sees Goliath as someone who is not just attempting to offend the army of Saul, but the armies of the Living God. David understood that they were fighting for the king, yes, but

---

[27] 1 Sam. 17:4-7
[28] 1 Sam. 17:23-26

the king, in David's eyes, was not just limited to an earthly man by the name of Saul…it was God Himself that was ultimately King in David's heart.

David receives his first test after arriving at the valley of Elah and inquiring of the prize for the giant, Goliath. David's oldest brother Eliab becomes furious with David because he thinks that, in pride, David has come down to the front line of the battle. He questions David and attempts to insult him and remind him of his insignificance in saying, "Why did you come down here? And with whom have you left those few sheep in the wilderness? I know your pride and the insolence of your heart, for you have come down to see the battle." David responded with, "What have I done now? Is there not a cause?" And those around him seconded that of what his oldest brother had already said.[29]

Is there not a cause? David's line of questioning was revealing the lack of passion in the hearts of those around him. David's passion for God was bringing to surface the complacency in the hearts of the men that surrounded him on the battlefront. David didn't see the fight as something that was for the glory of Saul, but rather he was willing to stand and contend for the glory of God to prevail.

---

[29] 1 Sam. 17:28-30 (NKJV)

Because of David's apparent courage the men brought him before King Saul. David said to Saul, "Let no man's heart fail because of him (Goliath); your servant will go and fight with this Philistine." And Saul responded, "You are not able to go against this Philistine to fight with him; for you are a youth, and he a man of war from his youth."[30] Isn't it something that as soon as you find the courage to step out and believe God to do something great that those around you, whom you would have hoped would be the ones to fuel what God is doing in you, are the ones that attempt to sidetrack you, derail you, and remind you of why you shouldn't be qualified for the moment? If David had not been secure in the Lord this could have been a major hurdle; but it was not.

The wilderness connects us with God in a way that leaves an indelible mark on us for the rest of our days. David was not relying on empty courage with hopeful expectations that God would come through for him. David was rallying present strength by reflecting on past victories. We know this to be true because David tells Saul, "Your servant used to keep his father's sheep, and when a lion or a bear came and took a lamb out of the flock, I went out after it and struck it, and delivered the lamb from its mouth; and when it arose against me, I caught it by its beard, and struck and killed it. Your servant had killed

---

[30] 1 Sam. 17:31-33 (NKJV)

both lion and bear; and this uncircumcised Philistine will be like one of them, seeing he has defied the armies of the living God." Moreover David said, "The Lord, who delivered me from the paw of the lion and from the paw of the bear, He will deliver me from the hand of this Philistine."[31]

David is absolutely certain that God will come through for him. David has harnessed the power of reflection. Reflecting on past victories produces present strength.

Reflecting on past victories produces present strength.

You may find yourself in a place, like David, where what is in front of you seems too big to handle by natural resources. You may be in a position that doesn't make any sense for you and you feel as if all of the voices surrounding you continue to rise in attempt to remind you why you should fail. Maybe you are faced with a giant hurdle that seems insurmountable. What do you do? Do you give in to the voice of reason? Do you bow out of the fight because you haven't been able to make sense of why victory is possible? Do you let the moment pass because it doesn't all add up on paper?

Absolutely not! You do what David did in the moment when I am sure those other options were tempting—you

---

[31] 1 Sam. 17:34-37 (NKJV)

remind yourself of the goodness and the faithfulness of God to you. You remind yourself of the times when God came through in impossible situations. You remind yourself of miracle moments in your life that you know were the Lord. You stand tall and declare that if God was with me before, He is with me now. If God was for me before, He is for me now. If God saw fit to come and deliver me before, He will deliver me today!

Don't allow the pressure of your situation to rob you of your ability to draw strength from God's faithfulness in times past. There is nothing too great. There is nothing too small. God Himself has said, "Is there anything to hard for me?[32] We too easily forget the great things that God has done in our moments of testing. Don't allow the pressure of your situation to rob you of your ability to draw strength from God's faithfulness in times past. We need to harness this power of reflection as David did.

WHO'S IT ALL ABOUT?

We need to take note of something very significant about this story with David and Goliath, and that is this: *David is not in it for himself.* It is very easy to read over a small line in this story of a comment that comes from

---

[32] Jer. 32:27 (NIV)

David. As he is about to charge Goliath, David says this, "This day the Lord will hand you over to me, and I'll strike you down and cut off your head. Today I will give the carcasses of the Philistine army to the birds of the air and the beasts of the earth, *and the whole world will know that there is a God in Israel.*"[33]

It would seem that David is motivated by the fact that this seems to be an opportunity to show the world that his God is real. David seems to be compelled into a fight with a giant for no other reason except to show all people that the God of Israel is more than just some fancy story that has been handed down for generations. David didn't make the giant in front of him about him. He knew it was about God…and it was supposed to be. Pursuing the giant was an opportunity for David to give evidence to the reality of God.

Have you identified who or what the giant in front of you is all about? If the Lord has not satisfied our hearts, we too easily fall into a place that makes the giant in front of us more about us than it is about Him. A heart that has not been satisfied by God sees Goliath as a way to promote self, rather than to give evidence of and exalt God. David wasn't attempting to tackle down the giant so that he could get his name in the lights. David didn't see

---

[33] 1 Sam. 17:46

the moment before him as a way to get his name spread around town quickly. David wasn't trying to become famous; he wanted God to be famous.

Who are you more worried about promoting? In what ways have you made the opportunity or challenge in front of you more about you than about God Himself? David wasn't thinking that slaying Goliath was the quickest way to the top of the company ladder. He wasn't trying to get on a bigger platform by running toward the giant in the land. He simply knew God, saw Goliath as a giant-sized opportunity to give evidence to the reality of God, and began to run.

Let's not lose sight of a very important takeaway from what is going on here with David and Goliath, and that is this: God used Goliath as a giant-sized opportunity to promote David. Goliath stood in the valley of Elah as a giant-sized window of opportunity for David. David was seeking to display the evidence of God and give glory to God. God honored the pursuit of his heart and promoted him in the process of it all. This is a thoroughly different thought process than the way that most achieve this platform of success. David identified what the giant in the land was all about, and because of that, God could entrust him with success.

When your heart has been fully satisfied, you understand that Goliath is not about you. When your heart has been satisfied, you don't have to worry about pursuing the giant in the land. The reason that David could so readily pursue the giant in the land is because he had already slayed the giant within. You should not pursue the giant standing on the outside until you have

You should not pursue the giant standing on the outside until you have conquered the giant standing on the inside.

conquered the giant standing on the inside. If David had not previously conquered the giant on the inside, any attempt to pursue the giant standing on the outside would have done more to feed the giant inside than to kill the giant on the outside.

For the one whose heart has not been satisfied, killing Goliath does more to feed me than it does to exalt God. For the one whose heart has not been satisfied, Goliath is no longer a giant-sized opportunity to give evidence to the reality of God, but rather it is a manipulative effort performed to gain something that I have always wanted. We need to understand that being deeply satisfied in God kills self-centeredness. We cannot live a life that is fully satisfied in God and put ourselves at the center. It is not a sin to love life; it is a sin to love our own life to the point that we cannot let it go to find satisfaction in God. If we are to ever be ready and able to pursue the giants in the land, it is of absolute necessity that we find this satisfaction.

God entrusted David with success. Can God trust you with success? When your heart has been satisfied, it doesn't matter if you are serving in the field with the sheep, in the field against the giant, or on the throne as king, because your heart is not in it for a title or an opportunity. This does not mean that because David's heart was satisfied that he wasn't going to walk into the fulfillment of the word of the Lord for him to be king. It just means that he was settled in the reality that it was up to God to bring Him in to what He promised him—not up to him to make it happen.

6

Decisions, Decisions

Romans 12:2

"Do not conform any longer to the pattern of this world, but be transformed by the renewing of your mind. Then you will be able to test and approve what God's will is—his good, pleasing and perfect will."

How do you know when to run toward the giant and when not to? How did David make the decision that day to pursue the giant in the land? Why didn't he reason that it was an opportunity for somebody else to tackle down? David found the courage to make a giant-sized decision that day. David had confidence, and that confidence compelled him into the field against a giant adversary. I find that making big-time decisions is something that doesn't come easy to all people. Big-time decisions that deal with the will of God for my life are the ones that have to be handled with the uttermost care and attention, right?

In looking at verse 2 in Romans chapter 12, the apostle Paul is making a great point about decision making. Do not conform to the ways of the culture, renew your mind and be transformed, and then YOU can test and approve what you are to do in life with God. Right? That's what I read. The way that this verse reads seems to reveal that there is a place of maturity where we can make decisions and live our lives in full confidence with God in the earth.

I would like to share a beautiful illustration that the Lord shared with me one day as I was sitting back and enjoying watching my daughter play in the house. I have a three-year-old little girl, and with being the parent of a three-year-old come decisions that I have to make for her because she is not old enough, or mature enough, right now to be able to handle her life as she would want to. If it were up to her, she would eat ice cream or chocolate, her two clear favorites, for breakfast every morning. If it were up to her, she would get to stay up really late every night, while eating ice cream and chocolate! So with that said, I decide what she wears; I decide what and when she eats; I decide when she is going to take a bath and how long that bath is going to be; I decide if she is going to have a chance to see her friends every day or not. My wife and I pretty much make all of her decisions for her in life at this point, and that is the way things need to be right now because of her age and level of maturity.

However, there is going to come a point in my daughter's life when she is not going to need me to handle all of these decisions for her. There is going to come a moment when she grows up and matures beyond the point of needing her mother and me to micromanage her life. At some point in her development I am going to release the control of her life to her and trust that all the years that I have spent influencing her are going to surface in her life and cause her to live a certain way. I am praying that the influence of her father is going to cause her to become a certain thing, which in turn will lead her to do certain things in and with her life.

At that point in life, I believe that she is going to live out of who she is; her identity will drive her life. She will be able to live from a place of identity and truly pursue the desires of her heart. She won't have to chase certain things in life in order to gain acceptance; she will be working from a place of being accepted by her father. She won't have to pursue things in life in order to feel loved; she will be going into life's decisions full of the love of her father. There won't be a need for her to attempt to find value in the insignificant things that will fade. She will have already realized her value in life by the years of influence imparted to her by her father. I don't want my daughter to have to make decisions for the wrong reasons, and I also don't want her to be afraid to live her life and pursue her heart. We must be true to our hearts; the only way to be true to our heart is to be settled first in identity.

Are you afraid to live your life? Are you intimidated by the thought of making decisions? What I find is that most people have been trained in fear when it comes to making decisions and living out their lives with God. They have been trained to believe that there is only one perfect and acceptable decision to make in each and every circumstance before them, and anything other than what is called "the perfect will of God" is going to throw off the entire plan of the universe as to how it should unfold.

Now I am not talking about silly stuff, i.e., what to wear today, what to eat for breakfast, or what route to take to work or school. These are all pretty much easy-to-make selections. But what about decisions that seem to carry more weight than these? For example: Should I sell all that I own and move to a foreign country in order to preach the Gospel to lost people groups? Should I marry the person that I've been dating now? What career path is it that God has for me? Should I start the ministry or not? Should I start the business? What university should I attend for the degree? Is it really the right time for me to move halfway across the United States and begin church planting in a city that I've never been to or have any connection with? These are decisions that seem to carry a bit more weight than the others mentioned previously.

I want to encourage you that the Father does not want you to be afraid to live your life. You are not supposed to be deathly afraid to make decisions in your life for the fear that you are going to throw off the entire flow of the universe by making what may seem to be a bad decision. The Father wants you to live in such a way that you stay true to the investment He has in you and the influence He is having on you. You can trust the presence within. You are involved in a beautiful process of *becoming* with the Father, and it is out of this place of *becoming* that He desires for you to make your decisions about *doing*. Romans 8:29 says this, "For those God foreknew he also predestined to be conformed to the likeness of his Son...."[34] The Father has you in a process of being

> **The Father wants you to live in such a way that you stay true to the investment He has in you and the influence He is having on you.**

---

[34] Rom. 8:29 (NIV)

conformed to the likeness of His Son; this is a process of becoming more like Jesus.

We should find great encouragement in this process of becoming; if you are born again you are no longer the same thing that you used to be. You are not the same person that you used to be. You don't have to make decisions according to the same thought processes and ways of reasoning that used to dominate your thinking; you can be free to be who God made you to be and live out of the influence that the Father has had on you and in you. Second Corinthians 5:17 tell us that once you come to faith in Jesus you are no longer the same, but you are now a new creation.[35] It is out of this place of being a new creation that you are being influenced by the Father into becoming more conformed to the likeness of His Son.

There comes a place in living out your life with God where it is not so much anymore about right and wrong. For the most part, you have come to realize what is right for you and what is not. What should I give my life to and how will God be glorified in it? Is this now the dominant thought ringing within your heart? How did David know that he should pursue the giant? What was the deciding factor for David that motivated him to put one foot in front of the other in his pursuit of slaying the Philistine

---

[35] 2 Cor. 5:17

warrior opposing the army of the living God that day? We are not given any great piece of insight into the thoughts of David, except his confession of, "Today all the world will know that the God of Israel lives!"[36]

David took the pieces of information that he had that day and did something with it to glorify God. Sometimes it is easy to make a lifeline out of missing information. What I mean is this—we are not ever guaranteed that at any point or place in this life to have all of the information that we feel is necessary. How comfortable should we be with making decisions from a place where we might not have all the information we want? Can you trust the Father if the full blueprint has not been given to you? Can you begin to put one foot in front of the other if you haven't been given the A to Z as to how it will all unfold and work out? Many will justify their inability to move because of information they feel should be necessary for God to give them before they commit to the first step.

At times, the position of sitting and waiting upon God can be a justifying reason to do nothing about what we are faced with. Now, this is not at all to neglect the influence of the Father or time spent in prayer about decisions that need to be made; that is not what is being said at all. But what I am saying is that there may be some things you

---

[36] 1 Sam. 17:46

could possibly pray about and seem to not get an answer to because the Father is giving you an opportunity to live from the influence that He has had on you and the information that you have already received.

What are you doing with the information/revelation that God has already given you? How is the information/revelation that God has already given you causing you to live your life differently? When we know that we *are* something, we are more comfortable with *doing* something. We should find great confidence *to do* based on the reality of our transformation that has caused us *to be*.

A DIFFERENT DAY

The issue is one of becoming. The time that we live in is one where information has become readily available like at no other point in our history. At any moment, if someone wanted, they could jump onto the Internet and research any given topic, and within minutes seem to communicate enough information that would cause you to believe they really knew what they were talking about. The simple transfer of information would lead you to believe that the person communicating was a certain thing. Our culture has allowed people to pride themselves on the mere transfer of information. The simple transfer of information is what has been appreciated. Someone doesn't necessarily have to actually be the thing that they are talking about, as long as they can communicate well enough the subject matter that is up for discussion.

This is a problem. There is a clear issue here. The way of the Kingdom has never simply been about the transfer of information; it has always been about transformation. Jesus, in John 6:63 said, "The Spirit gives life; the flesh counts for nothing. The words I have spoken to you are spirit and they are life." Jesus is not talking about the basic transfer of information here.

There is a big difference between walking around with head knowledge about a subject and then actually having walked through the process of life that has caused you to become the thing that you are talking about. Being faithful to the process of becoming gives you substance. The issue is this: when we have simply satisfied ourselves by just knowing the right things to say and we haven't made the decisions to commit ourselves to the processes of life that actually prove us to be the thing we believe, we end up deeply disappointed. We end up disappointed because now I know the right things to say, and although they may sound right, they are not producing in my life because all it is is a proper head knowledge. My head knowledge creates a false reality that I can take rest in if I am not intentional in my effort to press forward in this process of becoming.

The Pharisees had an image of reality that they upheld by knowing the right things to say and do in moments when it was called for. However, the reality is that they were not even the things that they claimed to be. Jesus exposed their bankrupt condition when He said plainly, "Woe to you teachers of the law and Pharisees, you hypocrites! You are like whitewashed tombs, which look beautiful on the outside but on the inside are full of the bones of the dead and everything unclean."[37] There is a great danger in satisfying yourself with having the right information. Being a carrier of the right information does not mean that you have given yourself to the process of transformation.

When all you have is the transfer of information, without the reality of Spirit and life, nobody leaves changed.

We must not satisfy our hearts on the simple transfer of information. Jesus was not after just the beautiful articulation of truth. He was the truth and therefore was able to speak in a way that changed the lives of whom His words touched. "The words I give you are Spirit and they are life"; this was a reality. You could not encounter the words of Jesus and leave the same. When all you have is the transfer of

---

[37] Matt. 23:27

information, without the reality of Spirit and life, nobody leaves changed.

People may leave having their emotions moved; people may leave in awe of the knowledge that you possess or the amount of study that you have given yourself to; people may even leave motivated or charged about living in a certain direction; but there will not have been a radical shift in the heart to move people toward the process of being transformed into the image of the Son. This must be our desire. We must not satisfy ourselves with simply knowing what we should say in certain moments. We must be real. We must desire the Spirit and life to be released from our lives. We must give ourselves to the process of transformation.

7

Water Walkers

Matthew 14:28-29

"Lord, if it's you," Peter replied, "tell me to come to you on the water." "Come," he said. Then Peter got down out of the boat, walked on the water and came toward Jesus.

Peter walked on the water. It was not humanly possible. It should not have happened. Yet, Peter trusted in the word of the Lord enough to step outside of his reasoning and the history of human accomplishment up until that moment in order to pursue Jesus upon the top of the water. Isaiah tells us that every word God

God is faithful to bring about the things He speaks to us if we will continue to trust Him. sends forth will not return to Him void, but will accomplish what He desires and achieve every purpose for which He sends it.[38] God is faithful to bring about the things He speaks to us if we will continue to trust Him. I would like to highlight some key takeaways from this story.

Why only Peter? The Bible says that all of the disciples were in the boat together. They were all there. All twelve. Why was it that only Peter was willing to recognize the voice of Jesus and attempt what none of the others seemed to be interested in? They had all walked with Jesus for about the same amount of time. The level of familiarity with His voice should have been the same. What was it about Peter that in the moment allowed him to become a part of history?

I believe he was willing! We tend to underestimate willingness for the Lord. You can teach someone the facts. You can show them the way. But you cannot teach passion. Passion is the key ingredient to willingness. You cannot teach someone to want it. You cannot give someone the desire. There will be times in life when you

---

[38] Isa. 55:11

are involved with someone and you will want something more for them than they may want it for themselves. Passion is what sets people apart. Passion produces willingness. Willingness introduces people to history-making moments in life. Peter was willing. Peter did what no other man had ever done.

One of the incredible things about Peter's willingness is that he was willing to leave the boat they were floating in. "What's the big deal?" you may be asking. Peter leaving the boat is a big deal. The boat represents something that was man-made. Many of them were proficient in the art of fishing and knew a great deal about boats, I am sure. The boat was going to continue to float whether or not Jesus had walked past them or gotten in. The boat is a representation of something that had been built with human hands that they could trust in.

The boat represents a life well crafted by the hands of the flesh and sustained by human reasoning and ability. Yet, when Peter saw Jesus and heard, "Come," he was willing to abandon his safe place and venture off into the water to where Jesus was. We must ask ourselves at this point, is the life I have crafted for myself solely established by human ability? Do human reasoning and ability sustain the boat I am floating in completely? If so, we may need to look around to see where Jesus is standing.

Do you desire Jesus more than you desire a life of comfort? Do you find yourself praying more for a life of safety or a life of significance? The moment Peter heard Jesus say, "Come," he decided the invitation of Jesus was enough for him to abandon all that was safe and comfortable in the moment.

Peter didn't think about what was being said. Now, I don't want to read anything into the text, but can you imagine what was being said in the moment that Peter was making his decision to cross the top of the boat and place his feet upon the water? Do you think the other disciples were cheering him along? Do you think that Peter's passion for Jesus was something that was celebrated in the moment he decided to respond? We do not have record of anything being said, but neither do we have record of it being a concern for Peter. Peter seems to be fixed on Jesus in the moment, and his fixation provides the entire context he needs to respond in faith. What do you need to respond in faith?

I find it interesting that Peter didn't consult any of the others standing in the boat with him as to whether or not they thought what he was thinking about doing was possible or not. Why didn't Peter lean over to John and ask, "Hey, John, what do you think about that word that Jesus just gave to me, bro?" Why not call Matthew over and say something like, "What do you think will happen if I really put my feet out on the water, Matthew? Will I sink? Will I float?" Or to Bartholomew he could have said something like, "We've seen Him do some pretty incredible things so far. Do you think I can trust Him this time?" None of this is present in the text, and I don't think that it happened. I believe Peter heard from Jesus, and in that moment his heart was quickened with the faith he needed in order to trust Him.

I wonder if the disciples discouraged him from going. I wonder if they said discouraging things as he was making his move to the edge of the boat just before climbing out. I wonder if they sat to the side and made fun of him as he was crying out to Jesus. In moments like that, it is those who are not willing to make the move that feel the need to discourage those who are unwilling to stay put. Those who aren't willing to do anything will always have a reason why you shouldn't do anything either. Those who aren't doing seem to have more time in order to discuss why doing shouldn't be possible. Peter didn't discuss; Peter did!

MY MOMENT

I had only been saved for a little over three months when I, for one of several times, encountered Jesus upon the water! I lived a very promiscuous life prior to getting saved. One of the results of this lifestyle choice was that I had contracted an STD at the age of eighteen. The STD that I contracted is one that doctors still to this day have not found a cure for, and that is herpes. The day that I came into this news was one of the most devastating days of my life. I can remember sitting in the doctor's office and having him look me in the eye and tell me that I had contracted an STD, and that now for the rest of my life I was going to have to take these little blue pills, Valtrex®, every single day, if I wanted to avoid major complications. The doctor shared with me that if I was ever going to plan on getting married that there would be no guarantee for me not to pass this to my wife. I would need to have special conditions in place in order to ever have children if I didn't want them to contract the virus as well. Life as I knew it was over. I can recall not leaving my house for weeks, being suicidal, and thinking about how my life had come to a place like this.

Fast-forward now several years, and I am twenty-one years old and just starting to walk with Jesus. It was a Sunday morning service in January of 2003. I was playing the djembe on the worship team for our church during an altar call because service was coming toward a close. Pastor that morning had preached a message about believing God for miracles. While I was sitting and playing, Pastor made the altar call and said, "If you would be willing to take the first step, God will meet you in your place of faith." It was in that moment that I felt God say to me, "Mike, I want to heal you." I didn't really know how to handle this. My immediate response, if I am going to be honest, was,

"Lord, I am not going to the altar so that somebody can find out that I have a disease." And so there I continued to sit…playing my drum…having this internal wrestling match with myself.

You have to understand that in the moment you are prompted to move in faith, the enemy will do whatever he can in order to fill you with doubt and unbelief. I knew that I had heard from God, and yet there I sat, afraid to let someone else find out what it was that I had. After a moment of this, God said to me, "Mike, you will never conquer what you are unwilling to confront." Now this was it: I knew that I had to get down from the platform and find my way to the altar.

You have to understand that in the moment you are prompted to move in faith, the enemy will do whatever he can in order to fill you with doubt and unbelief.

My heart was beating so hard I thought it was literally going to rip through my chest. I was afraid. I was shaking. I didn't even know what this moment that I was walking into was going to look like. Yet, in the midst of it all, let me say this, God spoke to me and told me that He wanted to heal me! I didn't even have an understanding of what healing was supposed to be about. I had only been saved a little over three months, yet here I stood at an altar responding to the word of the Lord to me that morning.

When the altar workers made their way around to me, the associate pastor stopped and asked me, "Mike, what can I pray for you about?" I was beside myself! They didn't ask anybody else that was standing all around me, and yet for some reason I get asked! I thought to myself, "Okay, God, so it wasn't good enough that I just came down here; You are really going to make me tell somebody about this?" I froze. I took an awkwardly long time to respond to his question, and when I did, this is what I said, "Umm, I am sick and would really like prayer."

What! Are you serious? I had heard from God, and yet there I stood, unable to stand up to the moment that was before me. They laid hands on me and prayed for me being sick and then off I went back onto the platform to sit back at my drum. I cannot describe to you how awful I felt. I was defeated. I sat there for a moment telling myself how pathetic I was, until, I had the bright idea to go back down to the altar and get in the line again. So off I went.

Standing in the line again, looking very strange to everyone that was helping on the altar ministry for coming back a second time, I waited. I waited and told myself that I was going to confront this thing and be done with it. I had no idea what was really going to happen, if anything was going to happen at all. All I knew was that I was tired of cowering under the pressure of this disease.

When the team came back around to pray for me it was the same person who I had just told that I was sick and had prayed for me the first time around. He stopped and asked me this time, "What's wrong, Mike? Should we pray for something else?" This time I responded and said, "I wasn't completely honest with you the first time. You see, I am sick but...." I was interrupted when he said, "Mike, you don't have to tell me. I already know!" They began to pray for me, and this is all I remember: it felt as if someone dumped a hot bucket of water on the top of my head, and it ran all the way down my body through to my feet. In that moment I heard the most beautiful singing and worship continued with what seemed like everyone in the building continuing to join in.

When I got up off of the floor all of the lights in the church were off and everybody had left. I looked around to see what was going on, and two people had waited for me. I asked how long I had been down because I didn't even know that I was down in the first place, and they said about forty to forty-five minutes. What? This was a serious shock to me because I had heard a multitude of people worshiping the entire time of what I thought was just a few minutes at the most.

After gathering myself, I went home. After changing clothes, I began heading toward the drawer where I kept my Valtrex® because I hadn't taken my pill that day. I opened up the drawer and when I reached my arm in toward the back where they were, I heard the same voice say, "Mike, you don't need those anymore." I pulled my arm back quickly and began to look around as if someone was in the room speaking to me. I waited for a moment and then reached my arm back in toward the pill bottom when I heard, "Mike, you don't need those anymore." This time I recognized that it was God speaking to me again.

I would like to testify that God healed me that morning over ten years ago, and I have never been the same! God healed me that day of what doctors said there is no cure for! Before, if I didn't take my medication for a single day, I encountered serious complications. Ten years later and I have been made whole in Jesus' name! I have a wife and two little kids, which my wife delivered both naturally without any complications, and they are both beautiful and perfectly healthy! To God be the glory!

One of the beautiful things about this story is that I had only been saved for a little over three months when God spoke to me and told me that He wanted to heal me! God pursued me to heal me! I didn't have an understanding about what healing was all about. I didn't even know how to pray for healing or if there was a way you were supposed to do it. All I knew was that God spoke to me and asked me to come and meet Him upon, what seemed like a water top, a place of impossibility, and I did. I am not anything special. God didn't favor me that day more than He does anybody else. I simply obeyed. Obedience isn't determined by the agreement of your external circumstances, but by an internal conviction that what God has spoken to you must come to pass.

What has He asked you to do? Where has He asked you to meet Him? Obedience opens the door to miracles. Many times we want the miracle, but we don't want to be obedient to what is being asked of us in the moment. What would have

Many times we want the miracle, but we don't want to be obedient to what is being asked of us in the moment.

happened if I never went back down that day for prayer? Would God have forced me to get healed? Would it have even happened at all? I don't know. I have no desire to attempt to wrestle through those questions. All I know is that I found a way to obey; I found a way to trust Him! And you can too!

8

Count the Cost

~~~

Philippians 3:10

"I gave up all of that inferior stuff so that I could know Christ personally, experience his resurrection power, *be a partner in his suffering*, and go all the way with him to death itself…" (*The Message*, emphasis added).

I have waited until now to talk about this subject because we had to lay the proper foundation before coming to this; the subject is suffering. Many have attempted to erase the beauty of suffering from their preaching, teaching, and writing by saying that it is no longer a relevant place for believers to find themselves. By doing so, they have robbed those who have adhered to such belief of the opportunities to be joined with Christ in the fellowship of His sufferings. I, however, would like to take a look at the experience of suffering, as it relates to living a life of obedience, and bring to life the beauty that is to be found there. Let me first give a definition of the way that I will use the term "suffering." Suffering will be used to speak of the process that God uses to bring us to the end of ourselves, the crucifying of our flesh.

If we are to talk about suffering as it relates to the will of God, I don't think there is any better place to look than Jesus. Jesus Himself was the visible will of God walking the earth among men. Yet, at the same time that we would approve that Jesus was the walking will of God, where did the will of God lead Him? That will led Him to do many great things for people: to preach, teach, heal individuals and also multitudes, and yet that will also led Him to the cross. Jesus was led to embrace a cross for the sin of the world. Jesus intentionally walked Himself toward the cross, picked it up, walked with it, allowed them to nail Him to it, and then hung up and out in the public and died. Let's say that again. Jesus hung in public and died. We seem to miss the enormity of that statement and what it really means about some of the places that God will lead us.

What significance does it have that Jesus hung to the cross and died in public? There were many facets to the work that was being done on the cross that day. The cross truly is the wisdom of God revealed in a glorious event. The cross was a work that was both public and private for Jesus. It was public in the sense that it was out in the open and visible to the natural eye for all who would be onlookers. It was private in that there was so much happening beneath the surface of what the natural eye was not able to connect with during its happening. And so it is with us; the work of the cross and the engaging of suffering in our lives will require us to embrace a public and private element.

Jesus didn't willingly embrace the cross in private and die in hiddenness, away from the ability of any or all to see. He was out in the open, in the public. Many of us are willing to embrace the cross privately. To a certain extent we can handle the way the Lord deals with us so long as it remains a work that is just between God and us. However, this was not the case for Jesus. As He hung that day on the cross, there was no question as to what was happening in His life; it was on display for all to see.

What does this mean? How does this have anything to do with you? I'm glad you asked. When desiring to live a life of obedience to God, never think that the road that leads to death is out of the ways of the Lord. In fact,

Jesus intentionally walked that path, and for the joy that was set before Him, He endured the hanging and dying in public![39] Jesus entrusted Himself to a process that required Him to embrace a great amount of pain. Jesus trusted in the goodness and faithfulness of His Father enough to willingly hand Himself over to death. Jesus was obedient unto death; the faithfulness of the Father would provide the motivation.

What is your motivation during times of suffering? Are you connected to the ways and heart of the Father in a real enough way that would enable you to hand yourself over to a process leading to death? You may not be required to actually give up your life and die literally, but there may be areas of your life that are very much so alive in your own strength that the Lord may be asking you to lay them on the altar.

Are you able to embrace the process of the Lord when it comes with a great amount of pain? Are you willing to walk the walk when it means you are going to suffer for it? Can you be obedient even where there doesn't seem to be an immediate payoff or reward for you to do so? There will be times when this is tested in your life. God will provide you with an opportunity to answer this question through proven circumstances that unfold in front of

---

[39] Heb. 12:2 (NIV)

you that will require you to confront what you will choose to do.

AT ALL COST

My family was doing ministry in central Florida as full-time staff pastors, and we were praying and fasting through a word of transition that God had spoken to us in the month of January, 2010. On November 13 of the same year, the Lord spoke to my wife and me separately and said, "Separate from all that you have and trust Me to put you where I need you." This word sounds great whenever you read it in the Abraham story, but when the Lord comes knocking on your door and says that it is time to go and He has not told you where you are going, this is a little tough to receive.

Three days later, on Tuesday, November 16, we both went into our jobs; I went to the church and my wife went to the corporate office of a large supermarket franchise, and gave sixty-day notices. We both gave sixty-day notices and had no idea where we were going. Our little girl had just turned one year old a few days prior to all of this. We stepped out of the boat. We stepped out of comfort. We stepped out with nothing but a word from God that we could not deny. Three days later, Friday, November 19, we received a prophetic word that, "Within twenty calendar days you will receive a phone call from a man that you've never met, to a city you've never been, and that is the door that God is opening for your family." Wow, the plot thickens!

To shorten a somewhat longer story, we received the call and ended up moving to the city of Charlotte, North Carolina, to join a team that was planting house churches in the university area. We arrived in Charlotte with hearts full of expectation for God to do great things, and God indeed intended to do great things. He just intended to do things that we weren't thinking He wanted to do. We had the hardest time of our life. We struggled in ways that we could not make sense of. We were forced to find God in the depths of genuine brokenness. We had expectations of God lifting us up; God had a path in front of us to bring us low.

I was working a job for several months when we found out that my wife was expecting our second child. It was a couple days after this that I found out the company I was working for was planning on shutting down the division in Charlotte, which meant that I would be out of a job. This is not the ideal situation that you would want after just finding out that your wife is pregnant. Now I have a wife who is staying home to take care of our one-year-old, pregnant again, and I am losing my job. Really? Not to mention that the job that I was working full time was only covering fifty percent of our basic monthly budget; so we were already in a place where we were believing in faith for the other half of what we needed to make it monthly.

It was at this time as we were praying through all of this that the Lord led us to partner with a missionary organization in the Charlotte area. This was a great blessing for us. We partnered with them two weeks before the official date that I was to lose my job. We were excited in the Lord for what seemed to be in front of us. We left that meeting and began to fund raise for our family in every way that we knew how.

Now, first let me say, we had committed everything we had to this. I was not looking for a job because we felt we were supposed to give ourselves to the work of church planting full time and fund raise so that we could do so. After six weeks of giving it everything we had and knew to do in fundraising efforts, we received the e-mail that contained the information of how much we had raised up to that point. Our hearts were flooded with excitement… that is until we opened it and saw what it had to say. We had successfully been able to raise twenty-five dollars!

After the ten percent that the organization took off of the top for an administrative fee/tithe, we were left with twenty-two dollars and fifty cents. We sat in our car in the driveway outside of our house and wept before the Lord. We were confused. We were disappointed. We were frustrated and tired of struggling. Either we had missed God or we had a terrible strategy. After committing ourselves to prayer about all that was happening, we concluded that we had a terrible strategy in place.

It was at this time of praying through all that was happening that we heard from God. God said to us, "I want you to walk by faith and let Me father you. I will provide for you." As if this wasn't enough, He also said, "And don't ask for a dollar, not even a dollar!" Okay. This was getting crazy. It would be hard enough to walk completely by faith and trust God for everything with the scenario that we were facing and especially to do it in a place that was far away from family and friends. Yet, though seeming to be an impossible scenario, that is what we knew God said.

If we are confident in who God is and what He has said to us, then it is not up to us to attempt to work out everything in our own ability and strength.

Why not ask for a dollar? Why couldn't we go around asking for help? This is what I believe it is; if we truly believed that this was a place God wanted to walk us through and father us, then it was not necessary to walk around with our heads hung low in the "woe is me" approach to life. There was nothing "pity party" about this. If we are confident in who God is and what He has said to us, then it is not up to us to attempt to work out everything in our own ability and strength. This was not a time for us to display how we could always make things work out in a tough situation; it was about trusting God, allowing Him to truly be our Father, and finding a place of rest in what seemed like a very difficult place.

During this time things didn't just magically work out for us. It was extremely tough. It brought us to places of unbelief in our hearts that we never knew existed. Sometimes we have to walk through a certain thing in life in order to find out what is really on the inside of us. There are times where our circumstances will be set up in such a way that it will cause certain things to surface in our hearts that we didn't know were even there. We confronted some ugly things, but it was necessary; it had to happen.

Our bills didn't stop coming just because we were walking through a process that was initiated by God. We didn't get released from all of our financial responsibilities because we had heard from the Lord. When we needed gas in our cars, we prayed. I can recall times standing in front of our refrigerator with my hand lifted in prayer to God and tears streaming down my face praying for food. Every bill that came in the mail we laid hands on and believed that somehow, someway, it was going to get paid.

When our little girl had needs, such as diapers and other regular things that toddlers need, we prayed.

This was not a cute season; this was a fight; a fight to mature, a fight to believe, a fight to add substance to who we were in the Lord. We were capturing depth in our walk with God that just couldn't have been added by sitting through a Sunday morning service. We were gaining depth in our life that just doesn't come by reading a book like this and being inspired. Being faithful to this process, embracing God in brokenness, and walking it through to the other side was the only thing that was going to get it done.

As you are probably already thinking, this was an extremely tough time for us. Tough, because up until this point, we had always had a certain amount of control over the way our circumstances were going to go with our finances. This was completely out of our control and in the hands of God. I can give you miracle after miracle testimony of God providing for us during this time. I could write another entire book about how we got to see and connect with God as our Father and provider during this time. Yet, in the midst of all of this, things never happened when we wanted them to. Things would always get paid, eventually. We were almost evicted from our house several times for paying late. We got disconnect notices for utilities, repo notices for our cars, everything you can think of, yet we stood our ground. We were unwilling to deny what we knew we had heard, what God had said. This was a season of just enough. We never missed a meal, we never had anything turned off or taken away, yet we never had anything more than exactly what we needed, and this was sometimes after the perceived deadline of us thinking we really needed it.

It was several months walking this way when we had the hardest month of all. We got an actual court date set against us for getting evicted out of our house; they were coming to repo our cars in a few days if they didn't receive payment; and several different utilities were getting threatened to be turned off. It was at this time that God brought to my attention a verse found in the book of Ecclesiastes that says, "He has made all things beautiful in its time."[40] This didn't make very much sense to us at the time because of where we seemed to be standing; it didn't seem to be all that beautiful in the moment.

Two days later my phone rang and I was offered a really good ministry position that would have involved our family moving to another city. Could this be what God was talking about? Was this going to be the opportunity that ended our "perceived" struggling and bring us into a place of stability? As soon as I hung the phone up with

---

[40] Eccl. 3:11

the man who called with the offer, my wife and I prayed. We prayed immediately because we didn't want to allow the thought to roam within our minds without asking the Lord for guidance. We prayed because we didn't want to have time to make this the answer that we wanted it to be by justifying it in light of our current experience. Upon praying, we felt as if we heard from God immediately, and this is what we heard, "Say no."

Say no? This can't be right. We were two weeks away from being in Charlotte for our first year. We were faced with the decision to resign our lease on our house, if they let us even do that. It would make a lot of sense for us to make this move. If we turned down this opportunity, it would mean remaining in a place that involved a great amount of pain. It would mean staying put in a place that we, for the life of us, could not figure out and make sense of in our minds.

Rewinding a year, there was a lot of excitement when we responded in faith to come to Charlotte and the adventure that was waiting for us on the other side of the fence. We knew that we heard from God in moving here, but we didn't know what our experience would be when we arrived on the ground. Now, we were very aware with what our experience was, and to be honest, it was one that we were praying would shift in nature quickly; this seemed to be a viable opportunity for that shift.

Let me just say that during all of the time we were living this way, it did not necessarily make the most sense to those that were looking from the outside in. People are not always going to understand what it is that God has spoken to you and what He has asked you to do. Peter looked into the face of Jesus and rebuked Him for saying that He was going to the cross.[41] And it was to this rebuke that Jesus tells Peter, "Get thee behind me, Satan! You are a stumbling block to me; you do not have in mind the things of God, but the things of men."[42]

Are you willing to commit to the process of God when those closest to you are attempting to rebuke you for your perceived foolishness? Will you go on even when you have to go alone? Will you continue in what God has asked of you when it defies all of your reasoning and better judgment? Will you stand with what you know you have heard? I could not deny what I had heard. I called him back and let him know that we would respectfully turn down the opportunity to come and join their team.

Will you continue in what God has asked of you when it defies all of your reasoning and better judgment?

----

[41] Matt. 16:22 (NIV)
[42] Matt. 16:23

After hanging up the phone with the gentleman that made us the offer, these words became very real to me: "Are You not the Christ? Save Yourself and us!"[43] These were the words from one of the men that hung next to Jesus that day on the cross as He was being crucified. Essentially, if You are who You say You are, bring Yourself down.

The man hanging next to Jesus on the cross that day could not fathom that if Jesus really was who He claimed to be, why He would choose to do nothing about what was happening to Him. This is the same Jesus that they had seen open the eyes of the blind, bring freedom to the demon possessed, give life to the dead, and yet in the moment that it would seem to matter the most for Him, at the moment where it was a life and death issue for Him, He chooses to do nothing, He chooses to hang and die.

This is important: He chose not to change the process the Father had called Him to. He chose to hang and die in public for all to see, for all to offer their opinions about it, for all to hurl their insults and their hatred, and He did nothing about it. Yet the beauty of it all is that by Jesus seemingly doing nothing, He was doing it all! There was more at work in the death of that Man hanging on the cross that day than the natural eye could

---

[43] Luke 23:39

see! God was working toward a greater conclusion than just the simple removal from a place of suffering and death. Without the crucifixion there could be no resurrection. Many want the resurrection power, yet are not willing to suffer and die for it.

Are you willing to hang in public and die? Are you willing to walk with the cross up the hill and knowingly let yourself be nailed to it and die for all to see? For all to offer their opinions on what is happening? For all to hurl at you their words filled with death and despair? For those who are genuinely concerned for you, and want you to do better for yourself, to plead with you to come down? This is the place that Jesus hung, on purpose.

There are moments and seasons of obedience that will require you to hang and die in public. How will you respond? What will you do when it is asked of you? I didn't say "if," I said "when," because it is the way of God the Father to conform us into the image of His Son![44] Paul said, "I want to know Christ and the power of his resurrection and the fellowship of sharing in his sufferings, becoming like him in his death."[45] The Father has more than enough ability to make all things beautiful in His timing, and sometimes that ability will lead us to live in such a way that causes us to unravel. Yet we must

---

[44] Rom. 8:29
[45] Phil. 3:10

unravel and be laid bare if we are to release the beauty of the Lord that is found in coming to the end of ourselves!

We ended up finding a place of rest in the Lord that was independent from our circumstances and things unfolding around us in life. We found a place where rest was a reality for us. Rest is something that cannot be faked; you are either at rest or you not. As stated earlier, trust produces rest. We had to come to a place where we were not just saying that we trusted God as Father, but that we *really* trusted God as Father. Active dependence was the expression of our lives. We stood on the word of the Lord when everything else around us seemed to be shaking and crumbling. We stood, and most times kneeled, in a place where to most people around us it had seemed as if we had "missed God." This process ended up lasting an entire year for us.

REST IN THE GRAVE

Jesus entrusted Himself to a process that led to death. Jesus trusted the word of His Father enough to transition from life to death and back to life again. I marvel at the picture of Jesus lying in the grave on Saturday. I say on Saturday because it would be the day "in between." Friday is the day that He would hand Himself over to a process of punishment and death that was undeniably torturous. Sunday would be the day that He would get up out of the grave and defeat death once and for all and pave the way for all that the Father would bring in His footsteps. However, Saturday gives us an interesting picture and some necessary insight into living a life of obedience and trusting the Father with the entirety of our lives.

Jesus lies in the grave on Saturday at complete rest. Jesus is at rest because He understands His Father is going to do exactly what He said He would do, when He said He would do it. Jesus has trust that allows Him to find a place of rest in the grave, knowing that the Father will raise Him up to life at the appointed time. His grace is enough. His faithfulness shall pierce the darkness like the morning sun in due time.

While everyone else that is surrounding the situation at hand has abandoned the cross and gone back to life, as they knew it to be, Jesus lies in the grave with great expectation and excitement. Jesus is filled with hope and expectation because He is lying there with a different perspective; there is a radically different lens by which He is able to view what is happening. Everyone else is certain that this is the "day after." Hope has been lost and all that they thought they had believed has turned out to be bankrupt and of no value any longer. They perceive this as the day after because Jesus, the one of whom most had placed all their hope and expectation, has hung on the cross and given up His last breath. It is perceived that He has been defeated. Excitement is gone. Hope deflated. Expectation lost.

However, at the same time that this is the dominating perspective for those who had followed Him, Jesus lies in the grave knowing that while many may believe this to be the "day after," it is also the "day before!" Insider information provides Jesus a different context for how He handles what is happening; His Father has already promised Him that He is going to raise Him up. Jesus is not lying in the grave scrambling and attempting to come up with a smooth way to work Himself out of this mess that He seems to have gotten Himself into. He's at rest. He lies in the grave unwilling to raise Himself in His own ability and at the same time He is fully dependent on the faithfulness of His Father to raise Him up by the power of the Spirit. What an incredible picture of rest!

You may not be lying in a grave, but you may be in a place where you have to trust the word of the Lord to you in a very difficult place that is bringing you to the end of yourself. How do you continue to trust? How do you continue to lie there and do nothing when it seems as if you have all the tools in order to produce a different outcome for yourself? Abraham had to find rest as he climbed a mountain with his son. Joseph had to find rest as he sat in a cell. David had to find a place of rest while he was running for his life day and night from a king that wanted his life. These men were sure of what they had heard. You have to be certain of what you know you have heard. You have to be settled in the character of your Father in a real way that produces rest in times when you should be falling apart. We have the ability to mirror the rest that Jesus found as He lay in the grave on Saturday by the power of the Spirit.

You have to be settled in the character of your Father in a real way that produces rest in times when you should be falling apart.

Stop squirming. Stop trying to dig your way through the dirt and raise yourself in your own ability. Lie back. Fix your eyes on Jesus, the author and finisher of your faith, and be diligent to enter into His rest. You must fight for rest. It is somewhat of an oxymoron to think that you would have to fight your way into a place of rest, but it is true. You must contend for rest, and when found, truly rest. He desires to be trusted. The process in front of you is not to distance you from Him; rather it is to draw you closer to Him than you've ever been. Though it may require a fight, it is a fight worth fighting!

9

Find Him There

Genesis 22:1-2

> Some time later God tested Abraham. He said to
> him, "Abraham!" "Here I am," he replied. Then
> God said, "Take your son, your only son, whom
> you love—Isaac—and go to the region of Moriah.
> Sacrifice him there as a burnt offering on a moun-
> tain I will show you."

A. W. Tozer said of Abraham that he was a man that had everything, yet possessed nothing.[46] Abraham

---

[46] A. W. Tozer. *The Pursuit of God.*

had many things, yet none of his things had him, not even his promised son. As it relates to seeing God correctly, trusting Him with our very lives and walking in obedience, I think it is important that we view this situation in the life of Abraham. God asks him to take his son, the promised son Isaac, the one that was divinely given to him by God through the miracle of him and his wife conceiving in their old age, to a mountain that He will show him in order to sacrifice him as a burnt offering. This is explained to us in verses 1 and 2 of Genesis chapter 22. All we are told next, in verse 3, is that Abraham got up early the next morning and headed off in obedience to the word of the Lord.

Can you imagine what that night must have been like for Abraham? Do you think he slept at all? Do you think he stayed up all night long and wrestled his heart out in prayer to God for Him to change His mind? We are not given any of the details of what that night held. All we are told is that early the next morning Abraham got up and started walking in obedience to the word the Lord had given to him. If you have children, which I have two little ones, I cannot even begin to understand how someone could commit to this, yet Abraham began walking in obedience.

Can you trust God when He asks you to lay down your promise? Think about this, Isaac represented the promise of God in Abraham's life. If Isaac were to die, then that would mean the promise would die. All of Abraham's hopes and dreams for the future promise of blessing were tied up in the life of Isaac; and God was asking for Abraham to lay Isaac's life on the altar and sacrifice it to Him. How could this possibly fit into the plan? What sense would this make? These are questions, which I am sure, Abraham must have thought throughout the night.

As the story continues, Abraham ends up taking a three-day journey to Mount Moriah with Isaac. As they approach the foot of the mountain, Abraham tells his servants to wait while he and the boy go up the mountain to worship. Abraham lays the wood for the sacrifice on Isaac and watches him carry it up to the top of the mountain. Even when Isaac takes inventory and realizes that they have everything they need for the reason they had come except for an actual sacrifice, Abraham replies and says, "God himself will provide the lamb for the burnt offering, my son."[47] What an incredible connection with God that Abraham must have had in order to look into the face of his own child, knowing what God had asked him to do, and yet still speak of the goodness of God that hadn't been revealed yet.

---

[47] Gen. 22:8

Abraham built the altar and strapped Isaac down, and as he was lifting the knife in order to slay his child, the voice of the Lord called out to him, "Abraham, Abraham!"[48] It is at this point that the Lord says to Abraham, "Do not lay a hand on the boy," he said. "Do not do anything to him. Now I know that you fear God, because you have not withheld from me your son, your only son."[49] Abraham then sees a ram caught in the thicket and gains this beautiful revelation of God and called that place The Lord Will Provide.[50]

There are two things that I find necessary for us to pull out of this story, of the many that are there to be had. First is this: Abraham really had to walk through this process. We tend to read through this account and skip over the actual process in order to receive the beautiful ending, yet Abraham really had to do this. Abraham really heard from God that He wanted him to sacrifice the very life of his only child, his promised son. Abraham really had to wrestle with that word all night long, and then get up in the morning and bring his son along for a three-day journey.

Abraham really walked with his son for three days, talking, sharing life, all the while in the forefront of his

---

[48] Gen. 22:11
[49] Gen. 22:12
[50] Gen. 22:13-14

mind carrying the word that he was counting down the very minutes he had left to share with his son before his obedience to God would bring them to a gruesome separation. Abraham really walked up the mountain and built the altar that he was about to strap his son down to. Abraham really strapped his son down to the altar and lifted the knife to end his life, HE REALLY DID IT.

The writer of Hebrews tells us that Abraham reasoned that God could raise the dead, and so in a manner of speaking, he did receive Isaac back from death.[51] Even though this may have been the way that Abraham was viewing the situation at hand, it didn't change the reality that he really had to walk through this process. God did not ask him if he "would do this." He asked him to actually do it; big difference. It wasn't enough for Abraham to simply give the right response to the question being asked. He had to walk through the process.

And not only did he have to walk through this seemingly gruesome process, but the Bible does not say anything about him being shielded from any of the mental or emotional stress that went along with this request. Is this something that you have ever considered? Have you ever thought about the weight of what Abraham must have had to carry during this entire process? Do not read

---

[51] Heb. 11:19

it into the story that Abraham had a special grace on him that shielded him from the enormity of the process; it is not there.

You cannot always determine what is the will of God and what is not by the way that you "feel" about it. Does God have to have your agreement in order for Him to have your obedience? Think about your answer to that question for a moment. This is important. Do you always have to be fully on board with what is being asked of you in order for you to feel that it is something that you should do? Is agreement a necessary component for your obedience?

If you are answering yes to this line of questioning, let's examine something for a moment. Are you going to tell me that when Abraham heard God wanted him to get up in the morning and begin the journey to kill his promised child, that he danced before the Lord about it because he was in full agreement with this word to him? Do you think that he was completely thrilled at the thought of murdering his promised child because God had asked him to do it? We don't get a direct look into the feelings of Abraham, but being a parent of two myself I can tell you that this would not have been the kind of word that I would have quickly wanted to obey. Murder one of my kids for God? Really? What good could possibly come out of this? What eternal kingdom purpose could there possibly be in this? Yet, even with all of the questions, all of the doubts, all of emotions that must have been involved with this, Abraham got up and obeyed.

We have to learn to come to a place where we trust the character of God more than the certainty of our circumstance. We must be willing to walk in faith. Abraham went through what was possibly the longest three days of his life traveling with Isaac and being obedient to this word. How many places have we chosen to be disobedient because we felt like we had to have a better understanding of the task at hand before we were willing to fully commit? How many opportunities have we bypassed because we could not reason it all out prior to putting one foot in front of the other? If we rationalize all of the opportunities before us, we will end up missing out on more miracle moments than we partake of. Abraham gained a revelation of God that day that he would not have been able to receive had he not walked faithfully through this process.

We have to learn to come to a place where we trust the character of God more than the certainty of our circumstance.

Obedience opens the door to experience. Many times we want to see God, but we aren't willing to be obedient to what is being asked of us in order for it to happen.

If we rationalize all of the opportunities before us, we will end up missing out on more miracle moments than we partake of.

That day with Abraham was not about taking the life of Isaac; it was about seeing where Abraham's heart was with the life of Isaac. Would the life of Isaac come before his obedience to God? This is what God was after. God had to know that Isaac didn't have his heart more than He did.

There will be times when you have to make the decision to keep walking in obedience simply because you know it is what God has asked you to do. You may have to sacrifice your understanding. You may have to sacrifice your agreement with what is being asked of you. What will you do? Will you arise the next morning and go? Will you respond? Your obedience creates moments to experience God. God wants you to be able to find Him in these difficult moments of obedience. He is waiting for you in the tough moments of life where it seems like you would never be able to get through what is being asked of you. He desires to walk with you through the valleys of the shadow of death.

Abraham intentionally made the decision to walk into this place with God. God presented him with the word and he responded. Will you? However, even though

Abraham was given the choice as to whether or not he would put himself in this place, what do you do when it comes upon you suddenly? Job gives us great insight of a man that found God in the depth of brokenness and suffering that came upon him suddenly.

Job chapter 1 tells us that the angels are coming to present themselves to God and that Satan comes with them. God asks Satan where he has been, and Satan tells God that he has been roaming throughout the earth, going back and forth on it. Then God immediately asks Satan if he has considered His servant Job, because there is no one on the earth like him. He is blameless and upright. He fears God and shuns evil. What happens from here is a little odd. Upon hearing God's testimony about Job, Satan determines that Job only serves God faithfully because God has provided for him and blessed the work of his hands. To this statement, God tells Satan that everything Job has is in his power, but he cannot lay a hand on Job.[52]

> **There will be times when you have to make the decision to keep walking in obedience simply because you know it is what God has asked you to do.**

---

[52] Job 1:6-12

From this moment forward begins a whirlwind of events that I would not wish upon anyone. Within what seems like just a few moments, Job finds out that his sons and daughters have been killed, his sheep and his livestock have all been killed, and his servants have died. In just a matter of minutes Job loses everything.[53] This is not like Abraham, in that God spoke to Abraham and he made the choice to get up in the morning and start walking; Job experiences a "suddenly moment" that literally turns his entire life upside down. Job doesn't get the word beforehand. Job doesn't have the chance to decide if this is something he wants to commit himself to. Job gets sideswiped by calamity in its greatest of forms.

Have you ever had one of those suddenly moments in life where you were cruising along thinking that everything was going great, and then all of a sudden out of left field it seems a curveball comes that just knocks you off of your feet? Maybe you went to sleep and all of your ducks were in a row, and then when you woke up in the morning you found out that somebody blew up the pond where they were resting. This is not a joke that Job is going through. Don't lighten the weight of the reality of what he is facing because you may be familiar with the ending of the story. Job is going through a life-shaking

---

[53] Job 1:13-19

moment, all at once, in full force, and it is in *that place* that Job decides to fall down and worship.

Job falling down to worship tells me that he is choosing to meet with God in this place of despair, this place of pain, this place that is more than what his mind is able to process or reason out. If you are anything like me, I attempt to make sense of all of my experiences. I try to cause all things to align into the direction of what and where I feel God is heading in the moment. The place that Job finds himself is not a place that I would want to attempt that. Where could He be going with all of this? Why would God allow this to happen?

The beauty of this is that although I am sure those thoughts wandered through Job's mind, he didn't blame God for what was happening in the moment and choose to distance himself. He fell down to worship. He wasn't bitter with God for allowing it to happen; he fell down to worship. Have you found a way to fall down and worship in the moments of life that present to you great pain and struggle? This doesn't seem to be a moment typically associated with worship, yet Job falls down to worship. Do you have a real enough relationship

> **Have you found a way to fall down and worship in the moments of life that present to you great pain and struggle?**

with God that you can fall down and worship in these moments? Or is your walk conditioned upon things always turning out a certain way? Our walk may be more conditional than we realize.

I have walked through places in life where I have not had a clue as to what God was doing or why He seemed to be doing it. Have you ever been there? Places where all I knew to do was keep my eyes upon Jesus because everything in my life circumstantially was spinning in directions that I would not have chosen for myself. It is in these moments that I have prayed prayers like this: "God, if You just tell me where this is going, I can hang on"; "Father, if I knew what it was that You were wanting to do with all of this, I could continue on in this fight"; "Lord, if I just knew who it was that You were blessing by allowing me to go through this perceived storm, I could be okay in the middle of this."

Does any of this sound familiar? I know that I am not alone in this. Yet, in these moments, what I am really saying is that my obedience is conditional, conditional in the sense that I don't like what I am going through and feel like insight or revelation from the Father is a necessary component that He must give to me in order for me to continue to be faithful to the place He is walking me through. "I could be passionate, if I just knew why...." These are conditions. "I would walk with joy, if I just knew why…." More conditions. "I would continue to worship You, if I just knew why…." Conditions. We hold our worship, passion, and obedience hostage until God pays the ransom of information to us in order for us to be faithful to who we are supposed to be.

The awesome thing about Job is that he finds a place of faithfulness without any insight as to why he has to go through what he is going through. Have you ever considered this? Job does not get an answer from God as to why He allowed him to walk through this place of pain and struggle. Not one answer, yet Job continues to trust Him. Not one answer, yet Job falls down to worship. Not one answer, yet Job remains faithful to God. Can this be said of you?

One of the greatest ways to test our hearts and our obedience to God is to remove our predictable outcome. A predictable outcome is an outcome to a certain situation or circumstance that we have figured in our mind is going to happen as a natural effect of us performing a certain task or going through a certain process. For instance, if I start going to the gym to work out, I naturally am going to expect a certain predictable outcome if I am training really well and have a great diet in place. Or, if I am hired on with a company for a certain job and they agree to pay me a certain salary for every two weeks that I am working for them, I expect to get paid. Well, this is not an issue when presented in these ways, but it does become an issue whenever we apply it to our obedience to God in ways that have become distorted and have taken away the beauty of obedience in certain scenarios.

It is very easy to create predictable outcomes with God and then be more committed to a certain outcome that we have created within our minds than we actually are in being able to find God in the process of it all and be faithful to Him there. It is easy to read through the story of Job, for those of us that have read through it before, and lighten the reality of his suffering in the moment because we know at the end of it all, God blesses him with twice as much as he had when he started. Job being blessed is a beautiful thing, and it is glorious on the part of God for the way that He blesses Job in this manner. The issue is not Job being blessed; the issue is how making this a blanket application for all of my experiences in life and constructing an entire theology around suffering always equating to a double portion of blessing in my life. Do you see where I am going?

The type of thinking that creates a predictable outcome from going through suffering and believing that I am working toward being greatly blessed with "double" of whatever it may seem that I have lost now creates this reality out in the distance that I have set my expectation and hope on. My hope is now that if I just hold on long enough, like Job, I will receive double for my trouble. My expectation now is that God must be working toward giving me something for my faithfulness in the moments of great trial and pain. If we are not careful, we will make more commitment to the outcome that we have created in our minds than we will to God. We will be more excited at the thought of being rewarded for what it is that we are currently facing than we will of being able to connect with God in those deep places of suffering; this cannot be.

If we are not careful, we will make more commitment to the outcome that we have created in our minds than we will to God.

The reason that this shouldn't be our thought process is this: we are not always guaranteed a Job outcome. We are not promised double for our trouble. This is not a predictable outcome that we are to live toward. Jesus coming back a second time for His body, this is a predictable outcome that we are guaranteed to experience; Job's ending, not so much. For some, this will be the case, but for others, we set ourselves up for extreme disappointment if we create a blanket application out of Job's ending for our lives.

Job determined what kind of believer he was going to be in the midst of the process that God had him walk through, and so it will be with us. Job determined that through the thick and thin of it all, he was going to hold onto God and trust Him. Although we have the benefit of reading the story from the beginning with the end in mind, Job did not have this luxury; and because he was able to find this place of faithfulness to God, we still glean from his life many years later.

OUTCOME-BASED THEOLOGY

Maybe you've bowed out of the race because everything that you were experiencing just didn't make sense to you. It is possible that someone taught you that if you have God involved in your circumstance, that you should always have a certain outcome. This is false and it is not the same Bible that I read. We can be given to an "outcome-based theology" in which we base our view of God upon what our experiences are. We will have times out in the wilderness where God will not perform for us at our every beckoning call or request. The way that we handle these times in our life will determine what kind of believer we either will be or won't be.

This is what I mean: When you live with an "outcome-based theology," what you are saying, maybe not verbally but definitely with your thoughts, by living this way is that who God is is completely dependent upon what the outcomes are in your life. If you have a positive outcome in life, then God is good and He cares. If you end up with a negative outcome in life, in order not to have to confront the negative outcome, we go back and look at the process to see where we messed up or how we missed it; because if God is truly with me like I say He is with me, then I should not have had to deal with a certain outcome. A theology like this tells me that if I walk with God, I will never lose a job. If I walk with God, I will always be in a position of financial wealth and gain. If I walk with God, because of who God is, then I should never have to confront certain outcomes in life—this is wrong, and once again, it is not the same Bible that I read.

Many who have genuinely believed have been shipwrecked by this style of thinking. We see it happen all the time. People come to faith because someone told them that God was going to give them everything they ever desired and that life was going to be a walk through the tulips, and yet when they are confronted with the hard reality that is life sometimes, they have no way to interpret what they are experiencing because of what someone told them their outcome was always going to be. And then to make it even worse, when people who hold to this type of thought do encounter negative things in life, rather than going back and dealing with the false thought process that they have had in place the entire time, they turn it on the individuals that are involved and come up with ways to justify their own thinking by then putting the blame on the person(s) involved.

People that are given to this type of thinking will say things to people that encounter negative things in life like, "You must have had sin in your life. Go back and find out what it is in you that is keeping God from moving," like Job's friends, or, "You must not have had enough faith in order for God to do what you were asking Him to do or work out the situation in the way that you desired." Are you kidding me? It is for reasons like this that many have turned away and abandoned a faith that at one point was very genuine.

What brings us to the place in our thinking that we really believe we are going to reach some level in God that is going to make us exempt from having to live life like everybody else around us? Now, I am not saying that we are to expect bad things to happen to us or that we are to continually live in a place that is negative and depleted, but we have got to get it together. A perfect example of this is found in the Gospel of Mark chapter 7. Let me set the stage for what is about to happen for a moment: John the Baptist has spent his entire life preparing the way for Jesus to be revealed; he even says of himself that he is a forerunner, or a voice crying out in the wilderness making ready the way of the Lord.[54] John has emptied his entire life into being obedient to the call of God upon his life; he has been faithful even when it wasn't convenient,

---

[54] Mark 1:3 (NIV)

even when it hurt, even when it was seen as a setback for his advancing in the culture/society at large around him. Nevertheless, he was faithful.

John has been preaching a message of repentance out by the river Jordan waiting for Jesus' coming. One day while John is baptizing people in the River, Jesus comes walking up with the request to be baptized. John, in his sincere humility before Jesus, says that the roles should surely be reversed and it is he that should be baptized by Jesus. Jesus insists with the process so that the Scriptures may be fulfilled. At this moment something extraordinary happens. The heavens are opened and the voice of the Father declares, "This is my Son, in whom I am well pleased," and the presence of the Holy Spirit descends upon Jesus in the form of a dove.[55] Talk about a moment in life that would have such an incredible impact on you that you would never have to doubt the person of Jesus again; and not to mention something that you would probably never ever be able to forget!

However, it is funny how soon we forget. When you read through the text and come down through the story, John the Baptist ends up sitting in prison for his obedience. Definitely not the outcome he expected for serving Jesus and emptying his life into preparing a way for Him

---

[55] Mark 1:11

to be revealed. And it is while he is sitting in a prison cell—and let's not forget a minor detail of the story, he's waiting to be beheaded—that he sends his disciples to Jesus to ask Him if he is the one that they have been waiting for or not.[56] This seems like a legitimate question to ask given the circumstances that he is facing, doesn't it?

The part of the story that really impacts me is Jesus' response to the disciples when they reach Him. Jesus looks at them and gives them these words, "Go back to John and report what you have seen and heard: the blind receive sight, the lame walk, those who have leprosy are cured, the deaf hear, the dead are raised, and the good news is preached to the poor."[57] Maybe you don't read the Bible the same way that I do at times, but this doesn't seem like a logical response on Jesus' part. They are coming to ask Him if He is really the Son of God as many believe, including who John, who is sitting in prison, believes Him to be, and He tells them to go back and report to John of all the great miracles and things that are happening all around him.

What? The issue that John is having is not if Jesus is capable of performing miracles. The issue is that if He is fully capable of performing miracles for people that are in need, how is he going missed and unattended to? Many

---

[56] Luke 7:19 (NIV)
[57] Luke 7:22 (NIV)

of those that Jesus is reaching out to, or responding to when they come to Him, are those that He is meeting for the first time; and some don't even have faith! This is an outrage! This is what is causing John the Baptist to be bent out of shape over his current positioning in life. He has spent his entire life paving the way for Jesus, and now that He is on the scene, John ends up sitting in a prison cell isolated and left to die? This does not seem to add up. This cannot really be the way that things are supposed to go. Surely, if Jesus were who He says He is, He would come to rescue John for all of his hard work and faithfulness, right?

The next words out of the mouth of Jesus are shocking. Jesus finishes His prior statement about the miracles with this, "Blessed is he who does not take offense at Me."[58] How does this fit into what it is that John is trying to ask through the disciples? It doesn't even really seem as if Jesus has given them the respect of addressing the question they asked directly—or does He? There is a powerful truth revealed in the answer that Jesus gives to the question of John that is surfacing through the mouths of the disciples, and it is this: I am not coming to rescue you John, and does that offend you?

Jesus was laying it all out on the line for what type of believer John was going to have to decide to be. This is

---

[58] Luke 7:23 (NASB)

where John's understanding and view of Jesus was being fervently tested, and we know that this is the case because he even sends his disciples to ask Jesus if He really is who He says He is. This is the same John that baptized Jesus. This is the same John that was a part of the crowd that day the heavens opened and the Father's voice came from heaven and the presence of the Holy Spirit in the form of a dove descended to rest upon Jesus. This is the same John now full of doubt because of what he is experiencing in life.

It is easy to read through the story and want to place a judgment on John for falling into unbelief and wanting to question the very identity of Jesus. But John just seems to be expressing in his actions the very same principle of "outcome-based theology" that we have been discussing. John could not connect himself with a certain outcome because of the belief system that he had in place. John's revelation wouldn't allow him to end up in his situation. John's situation had become a serious adversary to his revelation, and if we are not careful, we will fall into the very same place as John when we experience outcomes in life that we cannot reason out or fit into our belief system of who Jesus should be and what He should be doing.

When our experiences fall short of our expectations, we are in for a hard letdown. But maybe that is the issue that we need to be dealing with—expectations, expectations of who Jesus is and what Jesus should be doing. Jesus told John, "Blessed is he who doesn't get offended because of Me." In other words, "John, blessed are they who don't allow their situations in life to damage their revelation of who I really am." "John, can you still believe in Me, even if I don't come running to your rescue, as you would expect Me to do?" "John, can you still love me if this is where you end up and things don't change? Can you still believe? Can you still be faithful? Are you going to get offended and turn your back on Me if I don't do the things that you want Me to do?"

How easy it is to find ourselves in this place that John was in. We lose the job and wonder where Jesus was. We end up having kids that turn to their own way and wonder where Jesus was. We make investments and lose out on a bunch of money and wonder where Jesus was. We get the cancer report and wonder, *Where is Jesus?* We wonder where Jesus was because we have this unrealistic expectation that says that because I claim to believe, it should exempt me from the hard times in life. Because I believe, I shouldn't have to go through things that other people around me may have to endure. Where does this thinking come from? Surely not

> **Jesus never promised that this life would be easy; He just promised that He would be with us to the end of it and beyond.**

the Bible. Jesus never promised that this life would be easy; He just promised that He would be with us to the end of it and beyond.

It is very possible that you are either going through a very hard situation right now, or have gone through one at some point, that has caused you to have to determine what kind of believer you were going to be, a situation that made you really sit down and decide on whether or not you were going to be offended on behalf of Jesus. If you are dealing with an offense on behalf of Jesus right now, I want to ask you a simple question. What did you expect Him to do that He did not do, and what was that expectation rooted in? Battling through disillusionment is tough. Battling and not realizing that it is disillusionment is even tougher.

We have to come to the place where we are willing to admit that maybe we had some unrealistic expectations. Maybe we wanted Jesus to be and do something that He never intended to do. He had a perfect plan for John's life, and as much as we wouldn't want to embrace this, that plan included John sitting in a prison cell and being beheaded.

Are you willing to see Him correctly and follow Him wholeheartedly even when it directly contradicts the outcome you would be willing to fight for? Or are you serving Jesus with an "outcome-based theology"? Is your heart completely satisfied with Jesus independent of the outcomes you may encounter in this life? We must come to this place. If our devotion is continually based upon what outcome we experience, we will be no different from the children of Israel; we will be no different from the line of questioning that we find with John the Baptist. We must become different. We were never promised an exemption from the difficulties of this life. We were never promised an easy path. Our hearts must be satisfied.

10

The Authentic Life

Authenticity – The quality of being authentic; genuine.

John 6:15

"Jesus, knowing that they were coming to make him king by force, withdrew again to a mountain to pray."

There is no greater way to bring our journey thus far to a close than to discuss with you what is found in this last chapter, and that is: Living in Authenticity. Living the authentic life means that you have fully engaged your life; you have identified your lane, and that is where you are emptying yourself in obedience to this great race that we have all been called to run. You cannot engage your life if you are attempting to escape your life. What I mean is this: many have not found the peace and rest that comes from embracing identity, and therefore being able to live in authenticity, and so what happens is they feel they should be something other than what they are.

This stirring will leave us in neutral with the life we are currently living because our thought process will be something like this: "I can't wait to get into such and such a role so that I can finally begin living and engage purpose..."; "I will finally be able to do all of the things that are on my heart whenever I am able to have such and such a responsibility..."; "If I could only have this staff position or this title or this ministry, then I can be what God wants me to be...."

Let me say this: Identity is not determined by activity or environment; it is who you are or it is who you are not. If you need a special environment in order to be who you believe you are, you have not learned to live in authenticity; you have learned a behavior that works in a certain time and space. You are not all of a sudden made into something the minute your feet hit the ground in a certain environment. A missionary does not become a missionary when they one day end up in a foreign country.

Many think the answer is found in escaping their current life and are hoping for the day when they will have their life all lined up the way it is in their mind in order to truly live out the identity of who they believe themselves to be. This is wrong. God is waiting for you to engage your life in the now. We have been fooled into thinking that one day out in the distance we are going to have the great opportunity, in a certain environment linked to a certain activity, in order to be who we know God wants us to be. You have to engage your every day life. Your life of ministry should not ever exceed the life that you live with God. Woe be it unto you if you have a ministry profile that is greatly detached from the life that you live with God every day. The substance of your ministry cannot exceed the substance of your walk with God.

The substance of your ministry cannot exceed the substance of your walk with God.

We don't need more performers; we need people that have apprehended Him! We need people that have been wrecked by love, filled with fire, and are walking in great demonstration to give evidence to the person of Jesus by the power of the Spirit. This doesn't have to start in some far-off place that you can only envision in your mind; this is for right now and right where you may find yourself!

The only way to live an authentic life is to embrace who you are. Without embracing the "who" I am, I cannot fully understand the "what" I am supposing to be doing. If you have not found this place of rest, you will continually strive to run in a lane that you have not been invited into. John the Baptist is a man that found his lane. Jesus found His lane. Have you found yours? What is your answer to the question: *What do you say about yourself?* Many of the internal conflicts that you face in the area of identity are tied into this question.

Jesus is found in John chapter 6 performing yet another miracle. This miracle involves the feeding of the five thousand. We know there must have been more than five thousand people there on that day because it says that five thousand men were fed, plus women and children.[59] And so the opportunity is great, the crowd is large, and the stage is set for Jesus, and He doesn't disappoint. He provided for this hungry following this day in a way that is nothing less than miraculous. But what I would like to emphasize is not found in this portion of Jesus' activity, as great as it may be. What I would like to zero in on is what the Bible says He does next.

The Bible says that the crowd began to be stirred, and they were saying things amongst themselves like, "Surely this is the Prophet who is to come into the world."[60] The amazement and wonder of the moment was intense,

---

[59] Matt. 14:21
[60] John 6:14

and Jesus was the main attraction and discussion in the moment. Yet, the last verse of this segment, being verse 15, is what we need to see, "Jesus, knowing that they intended to come and make him king by force, withdrew again to a mountain by himself."[61]

Jesus was comfortable living in authenticity. Jesus was comfortable living in authenticity because He had connected with identity and knew who He was and what it was that He was put on the earth to do. The person who is walking in authenticity can truly abide in the Lord and therefore be at rest. Rest is not always a lack of activity. However, at the same time, you can have plenty of inactivity and still not have any rest. The condition of rest isn't predetermined by how much I may find myself to be doing; it is not taken from the busyness or lack of busyness of my calendar. Rest is found in trust. Trust produces rest.

When I trust that I am what God says I am and that I can be who He says I am to be, I can be at rest.

When I trust that I am what God says I am and that I can be who He says I am to be, I can be at rest. Jesus Himself said that He could do nothing by Himself; He could only do what He saw the Father doing, because

---

[61] John 6:15

whatever the Father did, the Son did also.[62] This was in response to Jesus healing the lame man by the pool of Bethesda on the Sabbath, a known day of rest. Jesus was busy working, on a day when there was supposed to be no work, because He said that His Father was working on that day. Rest is not about the subtraction of activity. You can remove all of the "work" and still have no rest.

Being able to recognize who you are also gives you the great opportunity to recognize who you are not.

Jesus was comfortable walking away from the moment before Him that day because He knew who He was. Because He knew who He was, He was able to walk away from an opportunity that didn't fit into the lane that He had been asked to run. Being able to recognize who you are also gives you the great opportunity to recognize who you are not. A beautiful illustration of this can be found in John chapter 1 verse 22.

John the Baptist is out by the Jordan in obedience, living and doing what he had been asked by God to do, when the Jews of Jerusalem send priests and Levites to ask him who he is.[63] The Bible is quick to tell us that John immediately lets them know that he is not the Christ. They

---

[62] John 5:19
[63] John 1:19

then ask him if he is Elijah or the Prophet, to which in both cases John is not afraid to answer and tell them no. Then they present him with a question that all of us will have to confront at some point in life if we truly desire to walk in authenticity, and that question is this: *Who are you? Give us an answer to take back to those who sent us. What do you say about yourself?*[64]

Have you answered this question? Have you ever even considered this question? Stop for just a moment and say this out loud to yourself: *What do I say about myself?* Until you come to a concrete conclusion in answering this question there will always be a present level of unrest within you. John gives us a great example of living in authenticity when he replies. John says, "I am the voice of one calling in the desert, Make straight the way for the Lord."[65]

John understood who he was, and he also understood who he wasn't. When they came to ask him who he was, they also presented to him what the crowd was saying about him. Some in the crowd must have thought he was Elijah, and some must have believed he was the prophet that many were waiting for. The fact is that these were not shabby titles and roles to fill in life that they were offering to John. Yet, even in the face of great roles, John understood his. John knew his lane. John had already come to

---

[64] John 1:20-22
[65] John 1:23

embrace who he was. He was settled in identity, and therefore was able to live in rest and authenticity.

I find it remarkable that John wasn't given to the swaying of the men that day to fill a spot that he knew he wasn't called to. Only a man that is truly at rest could turn down the opportunity for self-exaltation. John didn't have to give in to the opinions of others because he had already staked his peg in the ground of who God said he was. He was a voice crying out in the wilderness, and therefore he didn't have the need to try and be something that he wasn't supposed to be, regardless of how great the title, regardless of how lofty the status; he was settled, and at rest.

If you are not settled in identity, you will at times find yourself trying to fit your life into the context of what the crowd around you is saying about you; for the person who is not settled in identity is constantly seeking for the rest that comes from such a place. This seeking will lead us to continually need to find affirmation about our supposed or desired feelings about ourselves. John did not fit into such a condition. John was at rest with who he was and who he wasn't.

Those who are not settled into identity will give themselves to doors that open and opportunities that are presented to them in order to validate who they believe they are. The man who is not settled in identity, and therefore is not at rest, fuels his supposed belief of himself with the activity of his life and the opinions and persuasions of the crowd. John not giving into the opportunity to exalt himself gives us an appealing glimpse of what it means to walk in authenticity. Jesus withdrawing to the mountain by Himself gives us great insight into what it truly means to live out authenticity.

Jesus didn't need for the people to lift Him up as king that day in their midst. He understood He was the King. Understand this: The applause of the crowd will not always reflect the approval of God. Jesus' time hadn't come yet. There was a door opening in front of Him that was not in the timing of God. He discerned it; He avoided. The truth is that one day all people will bow down and acknowledge Him as the King. Jesus knew that this was something that He was entitled to, yet even though He was entitled to it, He didn't walk with a spirit of entitlement. A spirit of entitlement will not settle until the "I deserve" is fulfilled. Herein lies a great tension that must be confronted.

> **The applause of the crowd will not always reflect the approval of God.**

Can you imagine the scene that day? The people's excitement to rush to Him and make Him their king is arising, having just done a miracle; and yet instead of Jesus giving into them and allowing them to have their way, He withdraws to a place by Himself. What would happen if you were in a place where God was doing miracles through you and there were thousands on hand to witness the event, and the people wanted to begin offering you certain opportunities? Book deals? TV spots? Speaking at large popular conferences? Invitations to well-known ministries? An opportunity to acquire a place of status and fame? A chance to switch lanes and receive a greatly perceived benefit? Are you settled in your lane enough that you could turn these down and withdraw to an isolated place? What do you do in that moment? What you do in that moment says more about who you think you are than all of what your words may say.

Human validation can at times be a hindrance to the will of God in your life.

Only the person who is at rest in identity can walk away from the persuasions of the crowd and withdraw into isolation. Jesus withdrew. When your time of testing comes, will you? Human validation can at times be a hindrance to the will of God in your life. You cannot always discern God opportunities by the excitement of people around you. There is a huge difference between a *good* opportunity and a *God* opportunity. Jesus knew the difference. Do you? Jesus knew that His moment to be lifted up was coming soon enough, although it would look a little different than what the people that day had in mind. It would come with a crowd and plenty of voices lifted; the only difference is that they would be shouting, "Crucify Him! Crucify Him!" This would be the God opportunity that He would wait for; this would be the moment He would allow the people to lift Him up.

This is where we confront the spirit of entitlement. Entitlement can be defined as the fact of being entitled to something. In order to walk in authenticity you must confront the spirit of entitlement. For the man who is walking in authenticity is abiding in the Lord, and therefore is at rest. The spirit of entitlement rages war with the reality of rest in the heart of a person. Where there is a spirit of entitlement, there can be no rest until the "I Deserve" is satisfied. "I Deserve" fuels dissatisfaction. Being entitled to something does not validate a spirit of entitlement.

Jesus was deserving of certain things, yet He didn't extend Himself into operating out of a spirit of entitlement. In fact, the very opposite is true. The apostle Paul in Philippians says this of Jesus: "Who, being in very nature God, did not consider equality with God something to be grasped, but made himself nothing, taking the very nature of a servant, being made in human likeness. And being found in appearance as a man, he humbled himself and became obedient to death—even death on a cross!"[66]

---

[66] Phil. 2:6-8

Instead of embracing a spirit of entitlement, Jesus instead chose to be at rest and walk in meekness. Meekness is the rejection of a spirit of entitlement.

WHAT NOW?

Your life is not your own. We are all accountable to the words of Jesus when He says, "If anyone would come after me, he must deny himself, pick up his cross daily and follow after me."[67] Have you really emptied it all? Have you abandoned all things in order to follow after Him? I am not asking if you have physically detached from things or separated yourself from people, although some of those things may be necessary in certain cases. What I am asking is if you have surrendered your heart to Jesus completely. The things of this world are fading. All of that which seems so terribly important now will not be as bright and distracting when we stand before Him on that great day. Have you utterly forsaken all things within your heart to follow after Jesus? This is a matter of the heart before it is a matter of things that we may be attached to in life.

All of that which seems so terribly important now will not be as bright and distracting when we stand before Him on that great day.

---

[67] Luke 9:23

The rich young ruler in Luke chapter 18 gives clear evidence of a man that had attachments in life that kept his heart from Jesus. This young man comes to Jesus and asks what he must do in order to inherit eternal life. What I find interesting is that Jesus is very intentional about listing the commandments that involve exterior behavior that can be seen and measured: Do not commit adultery, do not murder, do not steal, do not give false testimony, honor your father and mother.[68] Without hesitation the rich young ruler verifies that he has kept all of these, and so by doing so, should be a qualified candidate. Yet, after Jesus has set what appears to be the standard, He takes a quick turn to get to the heart of the matter, and that is the heart of the rich young ruler. Jesus says, "Yet even in all of this you are still lacking one thing; sell all that you have and give it to the poor and then come and follow Me." At this the Bible says something that is somewhat disturbing to me when I read it, and that is this, "When he heard this he was very saddened because he was a man of great wealth and he turned and walked away."[69]

Please stop and take note of something with me: Jesus does not chase him down and change the terms so that He can change this man's mind. The terms are set. The line has been drawn in the sand. Jesus isn't after building a pretty crowd that is half-hearted and not set in their

---

[68] Luke 18:20
[69] Luke 18:21-23

commitment; He wants followers that have not loved their own lives even unto death![70] Quality doesn't get forsaken for quantity.

What has your heart? It is not that Jesus wasn't issuing an invitation to come and follow Him; it's that the wealth of the rich young ruler had a higher seat in the priority list of his heart than Jesus' offer. You will ultimately be obedient to whatever it is that you allow sitting on the throne of your heart. If it is your wealth, like the rich young ruler, then you will prioritize your obedience around your wealth. If it's your career, all things you decide to do will revolve around what will keep that intact. The rich young ruler missed out that day on a glorious invitation. Will you? Jesus knew the issue of his heart when the exchange began, so why didn't He just start there? Why did He allow the rich young ruler to think that he was on the right track?

We tend to examine our lives by the deeds that we do. We are prone to evaluate who and what we are by the things that we have done, accomplishments that we have, the charitable efforts that we have been a part of, and so

---

[70] Rev. 12:11

on. Notice that Jesus fed into this when He was beginning with the rich young ruler, and this was no mistake. This man was judging his readiness to follow Jesus by all of the external things, his behaviors, that he thought mattered most. And for many, they judge their accountability to Jesus' invitation to come and follow Him by all of the external things that may be happening in life; and like the rich young ruler, we feel that we have a pretty good grasp on being fully obedient to the call of God to us. But do we really?

Jesus said that even though he had all of his activity in the right place, the condition of his heart was still distant. If you are truly honest with yourself, is this where you are? Have you committed in all of the ways that have been convenient thus far but struggled to relinquish those things that have always sat atop the priority list? Jesus knows just where to probe to get to the real condition of where we stand. What is He asking you to do? What have you allowed to keep you from really being "all in" with your obedience in following Him? Is it worth missing out on all that God might have for you? Is it worth holding on to?

God is not looking for people that will go out and do a bunch of fancy things for Him. He is looking for men and women of whom He can do His work through. All things are possible *with* God; not just simply *for* God, remember? Will you be one that will lay down your life and follow after Jesus? God only needs one—one person who will love Him, one person who will trust Him, one person who will follow Him, one person that will make up their mind to burn for Him at all costs. The great revivalist of old, John Wesley, when asked why so many were attending his revival meetings, said this, "I just set myself on fire and men come to watch me burn!"[71]

God is looking for a person in the earth that will burn for Him. An individual so set on pursuing His heart that He can entrust Himself to them in a way that will radically impact the generation they live in. God is looking for an entry point. Will it be you? Will you pay the price? Will you set yourself toward Him with unrelenting passion? Will you lay it all down to seek Him? We are not waiting for Him. It is He that waits for us. He waits for someone to really commit. He waits for someone to really deny themselves. He waits. D. L. Moody said it best when he said, "The world has yet to see what God can do with a man fully consecrated to Him. By God's help, I aim to be that man."[72] With God's help, will you allow this to be the cry of your heart? Trust Him. Follow Him!

---

[71] http://quotationsbook.com/quote/27481/
[72] http://www.christianitytoday.com/ch/1990/issue25/2510.html

About the Author

Michael is a husband to Anna and father to his two wonderful children, Ariyah and Josiah. Michael holds an undergraduate degree in Practical Theology from Southeastern University in Lakeland, FL. After a love encounter with the Father that wrecked him at the age of 21 Michael has been relentless in his pursuit of the person of Jesus. Michael's heart burns to preach the gospel of the kingdom until men's hearts come fully alive to God by the power of the Spirit and burn with passion for His Son Jesus. It is for this that Michael and his family has determined to invest the rest of their lives.

The author and his family, left to right:
Ariyah, Michael, Anna, and Josiah.

About the Ministry

Burning Ones is the ministry of Michael and Anna Dow. The mission of Burning Ones is to preach the Gospel of the Kingdom until men and women's hearts come alive to God and burn with passion for His Son, Jesus, by the power of the Holy Spirit. Michael and Anna have spent several years in various pastoral ministry roles, church planting, and traveling evangelistic ministry. When our lives are consumed by Him, we become His burning ones! We are burning ones by experience and expression. We experience Him and then we express Him to the world. Burning Ones is not something that is exclusive to a specific time and space for us; it is life itself!

Website: www.burning-ones.com
Facebook: michaelsdow
          burningonesinternational
Twitter: @michaeldow